Twenty-Seven Dollars and a Dream:

How Muhammad Yunus Changed the World and What It Cost Him

Katharine Esty

For information regarding special discounts for bulk purchases,
please contact Katharine Esty via
Katharine.Esty@MuhammadYunusToday.com
Or visit MuhammadYunusToday.com

Printed in the United States of America.

Published by emerson books • Concord, MA

March 2013

ISBN: 0-615-79993-0

ISBN-13: 978-0-615-79993-3

Cover Design by Cindy Murphy, Bluemoon Graphics

Chapter photos not the property of the author used with permission
from Vidar Jorgensen and the Yunus Centre.
"Bangladesh Administrative" map used under public domain
from cia.gov. "Bangladesh in its region" map used with permissions
specified by commons.wickimedia.org.

This book is dedicated to my husband John,
who provided loving support, wise counsel, and
good humor throughout the writing of this book.
It is also dedicated to all those who are striving to
end poverty in the world and to empower women.

"Yunus is the most famous social entrepreneur in the world and a world class change-maker. He and the Grameen Bank have inspired hundreds of thousands of organizations. His influence goes well beyond Grameen's impact or even the field of microfinance. Katharine Esty's book is full of wonderful details that shed light on Yunus's personality, the development of his ideas, and how he has led broad changes in the world."

— David Bornstein, journalist and author of three books on social entrepreneurship as well as *The Price of a Dream about the Grameen Bank.*

"I found 'Twenty-Seven Dollars and a Dream: How Muhammad Yunus Changed the World and What it Cost Him' to be a page-turner, the details are wonderful and I also like the first-person touches."

— David Roodman, the Center for Global Development, writes a blog about microfinance and is the author *Due Diligence.*

"An authoritative account of Muhammad Yunus, the person, the serial entrepreneur, the visionary, and one of the most successful change-makers of 21st century."

— Asif Dowla is professor of economics at St Mary's College of Maryland and author of *The Poor Always Pay Back.*

"Katharine Esty's personal journey of discovery captures the essence of Nobel Laureate Muhammad Yunus, father of microfinance, and his pathbreaking work to transform the lives of the poor."

— Rosabeth Moss Kanter, Harvard Business School Professor and author of *Confidence and SuperCorp: How Vanguard Companies Create Innovation, Profits, Growth and Social Good*.

"This book tells the story of a true pioneer in the worldwide movement to empower women and in the recognition that women hold the key to fixing our impoverished societies."

— Alan Lightman is a physicist, novelist and essayist. He is a professor at the Massachusetts Institute of Technology and the author of the international bestseller *Einstein's Dreams*.

"Katharine Esty, an American social psychologist and organizational change consultant, explains and upholds the work and the legacy of this complicated, gifted man. Her frank and coolheaded portrait of Yunus, and her clear, perceptive assessment of the strategies that made the Grameen Bank thrive show not only what it takes to dream a possible dream, but how to make one real."

— Liesl Schillinger is a New York–based writer and literary critic whose work has appeared in *The New York Times Book Review*, *The New Yorker*, and *New York* magazine.

Table of Contents

Bangladesh in its Region

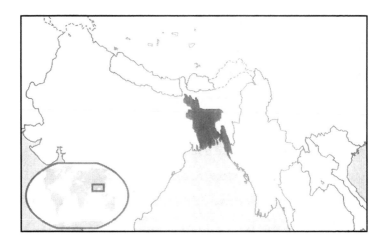

Bangladesh

BANGLADESH   Administrative Divisions

- International boundary
- Division boundary
- ★ National capital
- ◉ Division capital

Bangladesh has seven divisions.

Scale 1:3,500,000

NEPAL

BHUTAN

RANGPUR
◉ Rangpur

INDIA

RÂJSHAHI
◉ Râjshâhi

DHAKA

SYLHET
Sylhet ◉

DHAKA ★

INDIA

Khulna ◉
KHULNA

Barisâl ◉
BARISÂL

CHITTAGONG

◉ Chittagong

BURMA

Bay of Bengal

Yunus and Katharine Esty in 2010.

Prologue

This book began the day I met Muhammad Yunus in 1994. He became my hero on the spot because he was working to end poverty and he was focusing on lending to poor women. Now, almost twenty years later, Yunus remains my hero. I am still deeply moved by his lifelong struggle to end poverty, his success in bringing women into the financial system, his promotion of social businesses (which aim to make a profit and address a social problem), and his dazzling success as a master of change. Today, only about one in five people I meet know who Muhammad Yunus is. I want his story known to a far larger number of people around the world.

* * * * *

It was 114 degrees in Dhaka, Bangladesh, that May morning in 1994 when I arrived at the Grameen Bank to interview the Bank's managing director, a man named Muhammad Yunus. I had never heard of him. A guard in a khaki uniform stepped briskly forward to usher me inside. "Professor Yunus is on the fourth floor," he announced as he gestured toward a dark, cement stairway. As I began climbing up the stairs it quickly dawned on me that this was a building without air conditioning. The air was moist and it was so hot I was almost scared. I felt my cheeks turning purple and rivulets of sweat streamed down my back. I had never been so uncomfortable in my entire life.

I had been thrilled when Rolf Carriere, the head of UNICEF in Bangladesh, had asked me to facilitate a series of large planning conferences on major national issues. This was an exciting opportunity for me to bring my skills as a social psychologist and an organizational change consultant to the third world and to work at the highest levels in Bangladesh. But actually being here in Dhaka, with its heart-rending poverty, unbearable heat, low-lying smog, and the foul stench on the streets was not so glamorous.

My interview with the head of the Grameen Bank was one of six that had been scheduled for me for the day. I arrived at last on the fourth floor. A cherubic Professor Muhammad Yunus, standing at the doorway of his office, welcomed me with a handshake and a radiant smile that put me instantly at ease. He was dressed in a plaid tunic and loose-fitting pants—not my idea of banker's garb. I surveyed his office. It was nearly bare, with only a single wood table and a few straight chairs. As I launched into my explanation of UNICEF's planning meeting called Future Search, Professor Yunus listened intently. After several minutes, he responded, "The process must be owned by Bangladeshis. " I sensed steel behind the comment. I looked to see whether this was an unfriendly challenge but his warm smile suggested that was not the case. It would be some time later before I would understand his negative views of foreign consultants like me working in Bangladesh.

It seemed like his comment had ended my pitch for the Future Search, so I asked him about his work and with just the slightest prompt, he launched into his life story. He had been an economics professor with no intention of becoming a banker. But during Bangladesh's famine of 1973, all his theories and knowledge seemed useless. He wanted to reduce the suffering of people he saw all around him, and so he lent $27 to a few poor people in a nearby village. They paid him back. He discovered over the next months and years that the poor pay back their loans at astonishingly high rates—over 98 percent—and that credit changed their lives for the better. Now, Professor Yunus continued, 20 years later, in 1994, the Grameen Bank had spawned branches in more than 1,000 villages. "Grameen," I learned, means "rural" or "village. "

Yunus went on to explain that the Grameen Bank, unlike all other banks in the country, focused most of its efforts on poor women. It had not been easy to persuade women to become borrowers, but Yunus persisted since he saw that a loan to a woman was more likely to improve the lot of a whole family than a loan to a man.

He went on to describe the culture of a village in Bangladesh. Women are taught not to speak up and never to look at someone directly. Most poor women have never even held money in their hands. It is not customary for a woman to go to the market. For all these reasons, it took enormous courage for a woman to take a loan. And yet, his bank had been successful in attracting women. He explained that the Grameen Bank was now lending to millions of women in Bangladesh and his model had been adopted by many other organizations around the world.

As Yunus talked, I was spellbound. I wondered why I, a feminist and an organizational development consultant who was deeply concerned with social justice, had never heard of him. But more than that, I was profoundly moved by his story and what he was about. Here he was, a Muslim man focusing his work on women. That certainly shattered my stereotypes. Questions flooded my mind. Was he too good to be true? How had he been able to achieve so much? What was his back story? But what I knew for certain was that I had met someone very special and that I would never forget him or our encounter.

Yunus went on during the next twelve years to achieve even more recognition among those interested in international development and microfinance. My interest in him was reawakened when he was awarded the Nobel

Peace Prize in 2006 and I began my research in earnest at that time.

Since 2006, Yunus has faced attacks from abroad and, more importantly, from the government of Bangladesh and the Prime Minister. He struggled to hold on to his position as managing director of the Grameen Bank but was eventually forced to resign. Despite all the many attempts to discredit him and the loss of his role at the Grameen Bank, he works indefatigably to promote social businesses and to continue his war on poverty.

Yunus's life journey has been a saga of improbable successes, betrayals, setbacks, and conflict. It is a thrilling adventure story. It is also a guide book for all those who want to change the world and to make a positive difference.

Since I began my research I have come up with many new and different questions about Yunus. One in particular looms above all others and provides a major focus to this book. How has Muhammad Yunus changed the world, and what can we learn from him about how to do it? So this book is also for change agents who want to make a difference in their communities or the world and for all those at universities and business schools who are interested in learning more about managing successful change efforts.

Yunus and Taslima Begum proudly display their Nobel Peace Prize certificates and medals.

Chapter One:

The Most Prestigious Prize in the World

The news that Muhammad Yunus and the Grameen Bank were the 2006 winners of the Nobel Peace Prize flashed around the world in nanoseconds. Those who were acquainted with Yunus knew he would play the role of the Nobel laureate, as he played every role in life, in ways that were creative, bold, and controversial. They suspected that a man who had turned conventional banking on its head would probably do the same with the Nobel experience. But exactly how he would use this opportunity was unpredictable.

The critics began immediately to voice objections to the choice of Yunus. There has often been controversy about the winners of the Nobel Peace Prize. Remember the reactions when Al Gore and Obama won the prize. But the choice of Yunus generated a particularly prolonged debate and fierce opposition, not only about the man but also about microfinance.

Ole Danbolt Mjos, the chairman of the Nobel Committee, was already on the defensive as he announced the prize. He carefully explained the Committee's rationale for the choice of a bank and a banker and then went on to make clear the connection between poverty and peace. "Lasting peace cannot be achieved," he said, "unless large population groups find ways in which to break out of poverty. Microcredit is one such means."[1]

The Economist wondered whether the choice of Yunus suggested that the Nobel was "losing its luster." Tom Bethell commented wryly in *The American*, "Yunus must be the most widely admired moneylender in history. Since when did they give the prize to bankers that lend money at 20 percent?"[2] David Satterthwaite, CEO of Prisma MicroFinance, challenged the accomplishments of Yunus and microcredit itself. He wrote, "On this day of great celebration, we urge caution. Micro-banks currently lack the institutional strength to become large ('scaled') organizations due to unprofessional management, opaque governance and meager balance sheets."[3]

In Bangladesh, where Yunus was a hero and a favorite son, the news that he and the Grameen Bank had won the Nobel Peace Prize sparked three days of wild celebrations. Young men marched in the streets carrying banners, and fireworks boomed at night. Since Yunus was the first person from the new country of Bangladesh to win a Nobel Prize, it was a triumph for the entire nation.

Yet there were millions around the world who had never heard of Yunus— or microcredit, for that matter. Despite the fact that governments, universities, and organizations had showered him with more than 60 major prizes as well as innumerable honorary degrees, his name was not a household word. Of those 60 earlier prizes, seven were for achievements in the area of peace; others recognized his work in architecture, justice, freedom, innovation, technology, humanitarian leadership, and social entrepreneurship.

As Yunus told me years later in one of the hours I spent interviewing him, many of his colleagues at the bank him urged to spend an entire month writing his speech. The Nobel lecture, after all, would be the centerpiece of the ceremonies and an opportunity of a lifetime. Yunus was aware that the whole world would be watching, but he had supreme confidence in his ability to communicate his ideas. He told them, "No, I don't have a month. I don't have a day to do that."[4] With just a hint of pride, and with a smile, Yunus admitted to me that he ignored all this advice and prepared his lecture in a single afternoon, sitting in a hotel room.

Rather than selecting the top executives to represent the bank at the ceremonies in Oslo, Yunus chose the nine village women who were on the Grameen Bank's Board of Directors. These were poor, illiterate women who had never been on an airplane or traveled outside Bangladesh. All of them were borrowers and, as borrowers, both shareholders and owners of the Bank. They had qualified for loans because they were poor and landless. One of the Board Directors, a woman named Mossammet Taslima Begum, was selected to be the person to receive the award at the ceremony on behalf of the Bank.

Begum, by the way, is a title like Mrs. or Madame. Since many Bangladeshis have only first names, it is common to add Begum to a married woman's name.

The trip to Oslo for the award ceremony was a major life event for these women. Grameen staff scurried around to acquire passports for them and to outfit them with the warm coats and gloves necessary for a visit to Norway in winter. Since rural women in Bangladesh do not travel except with a male relative, a number of husbands joined the group.

Yunus invited many others to accompany him: key staff members, some of whom who had been with him since the mid-seventies, family including his wife, both daughters, and some of his brothers, and friends. All told, the entourage of Bangladeshis bound for Oslo consisted of 70 people. Yunus also invited Queen Sofia of Spain, who had been a long-time champion of microcredit and of Yunus himself. When it became known that she was coming, the king and queen of Norway also decided to show up for the ceremony, something they had never done previously.

There was fanfare and a red carpet to welcome the Nobel winners and the royal guests as they arrived at City Hall for the award ceremony. Yunus and Taslima

Begum, King Harold and Queen Sonia, along with the crown prince and princess, paraded into the immense hall decorated with blue banners and banks of bright red flowers.

Mjos, chairman of the Nobel Committee, dressed in a dark suit and white shirt, delivered the presentation speech in Norwegian. Once again he made the case for the choice of Yunus and Grameen Bank. "Since the 11th of September 2001, we have seen a widespread tendency to demonize Islam. The Peace Prize to Yunus and Grameen Bank is also support for the Muslim country Bangladesh and for the Muslim environments in the world that are working for dialogue and collaboration. ... Secondly, this year's Peace Prize places women centre-stage. Microcredit has proved itself to be a liberating force in societies where women in particular have to struggle against repressive social and economic conditions. ... Thirdly, and most important, we have the fight against poverty and for social and economic development. From modest beginnings three decades ago, Yunus has first and foremost, through Grameen Bank, developed microcredit into an ever more important instrument in the struggle against poverty."[5]

Then it was time for Yunus and Taslima Begum to receive the prize diplomas and medals. As Mjos placed the Nobel medals around their necks and handed them the diplomas, the audience clapped wildly and rose en masse to give them a standing ovation. Then the crowd hushed as Taslima began to speak. She stood tall and her voice was clear and firm. It didn't matter that only a handful of the audience could understand her words, spoken in a dialect of Bangla. Her presence beside the dignitaries and royalty spoke loud and clear. The poor of the world, the billions at the bottom of the economic pyramid, were no longer invisible. One of them had been awarded the most prestigious prize in the world.

Susan Davis, a development expert and a founder of the Grameen Foundation, described it this way. "So Taslima is one of those people we talk about: the poorest of the poor trying to use microcredit to lift themselves out of poverty. And she, like many of the other board members, was a victim of child marriage, married at nine. So when she spoke out at the Nobel Peace Prize, I just lost it. … It was the spirit of empowerment just ringing through her body. And for the first time, I think, the world heard a Nobel laureate who is from the poorest of the poor."[6]

The mood shifted as a gorgeous troupe of young men and women dressed in brilliant red and yellow costumes swirled out onto the platform and performed a traditional Bangladeshi dance, showcasing another aspect of their country. Yunus, the producer of this Nobel drama and a fervent nationalist, was determined that his country be known for more than poverty and natural calamities.

Chapter One: **The Most Prestigious Prize in the World**

When Yunus himself strode to the podium to deliver his Nobel lecture, he stood in stark contrast to Mjos and other Committee dignitaries in their dark suits. He was wearing khaki pants and a beige, hand-woven, traditional Bangladeshi tunic over his grey shirt. He began in Bangla, addressing the Bangladeshis in the audience and around the world. Asif Dowla, a Bangladeshi and former student and colleague of Yunus's, who was watching the ceremony on closed circuit TV outside the hall in Oslo, wept. The Nobel Committee was nervous about him speaking in Bangla. But Yunus insisted on beginning his lecture in his native language because the whole of Bangladesh would be watching and he did not want to miss this opportunity to address the youth of Bangladesh.

Yunus continued his speech in English. He declared that the presence of the poor women from the villages gave an altogether new meaning to the Nobel Peace Prize. The poor are rarely on podiums to receive recognition, yet half of the world population lives on less than two dollars a day. More than one billion people live on less than one dollar a day. He summarized the accomplishments of the Grameen Bank, which by 2006 had lent money to nearly seven million poor people, 97 percent of whom were women. In Bangladesh, he added, 80 percent of poor families had now been reached with microcredit.

So far the speech was going along much as expected. But then—a surprise twist. Yunus left the subject of microcredit and turned to social business. In this new kind of business, he explained, after investors get back their original investment, all profits are plowed back into the organization and used to confront a social problem. This, he suggested, would be a very powerful tool in efforts to eliminate poverty altogether.

Yunus was using his platform to go beyond the celebration of his past achievements. He was charting his course for the future. He concluded by insisting that we can create a world without poverty if only we believe it is possible. The speech had struck a chord. His use of many of his familiar analogies and images made it Yunus at his best, and a tour de force. But what made the speech really important was the announcement of his new mission and the new focus of his work to end poverty.

The next night was the Nobel Peace Prize Concert, which Angelica Huston and Sharon Stone hosted and where Yusuf Islam (formerly Cat Stevens) was a featured performer, along with the British pop band Simply Red, Lionel Richie, Wynonna Judd, Renee Fleming, and Hakim. But for Yunus, the magical moment came when his daughter, Monica, sang "O Mio Babbino Caro" (Oh, My Dear Daddy), an aria from a Puccini opera.

Monica is famous in her own right as an opera singer. Her mother, Yunus's first wife, Vera, had not wanted to bring up Monica in Bangladesh, and Yunus would not leave his native land. This impasse had led to a divorce, and to Monica's growing up in New Jersey. She took voice lessons from childhood, was trained at Juilliard, and has performed at the Metropolitan Opera in New York and at opera houses all over Europe. Yunus didn't see her for some years during her adolescence, but in 2004 they were reunited. Since then they have traveled together a number of times; Monica has sung at several concerts benefiting microfinance, and she has married another opera singer.

Winning the Nobel skyrocketed Yunus to fame and to membership in an elite group of Nobel Prizewinners that includes Kofi Annan, Nelson Mandela, and the Dalai Lama, to name a few. The impact this award had on him can't be overstated. He put it this way: "The prize made it easier for me to advocate for changes in relevant policies and regulations. Earlier I used to scream and shout, and not many listened to me. Now I am seen as a wise man, and even my whisper carries a lot more weight."[7]

Sitting with Yunus one afternoon in 2010 in his bare and chilly office in Dhaka, I learned more about how the prize had impacted his life. "The prize gives you so much respectability," he said. "Other prizes—it's never even mentioned that somebody got it. But this one, the day that prize is announced—every single newspaper in the world makes it first page news. And then on the following day there's an editorial on you. What you have done, and congratulations. So that immediately it opens up many doors. Where you have been trying for your life to have just a little opening—now it stands open for you. You just walk in. They welcome you."[8]

The Nobel Peace Prize was clearly a crossroads moment. Staff reported that the mood of euphoria at the Bank lasted for months. Invitations for Yunus to give speeches and attend gatherings poured in from around the world. And, yes, in later years there would be more awards and more prizes, including the U.S. Presidential Medal of Freedom and the Congressional Gold Medal. But this was the moment of glory–Yunus at the pinnacle of success. And at that time, no one could imagine that in a few short years clouds of distrust would gather.

* * * * *

I shivered in the cold, dank lobby of the Grameen Bank that afternoon in January, 2010. I was early for this trip's first interview in Bangladesh, which was scheduled for five o'clock. The sun had already set. Two guards in uniform chatted at the doorway. Their two cheap plastic chairs were the only furniture in sight. I would soon learn that the elevators on either side of the lobby were finicky, refusing to stop at certain floors and sometimes shutting down altogether. Straight ahead, painted right on the wall, was a twelve-foot-high mural of Muhammad Yunus's head and an announcement of the Nobel Peace Prize Exhibit in a room just behind.

Chapter One: **The Most Prestigious Prize in the World**

I followed the signs to the exhibit and found myself in the dark in the middle of a gaggle of six women who were slowly sweeping the floor. Seeing me, they smiled shyly, and one of them rushed to turn on the lights. I remembered electricity cannot be wasted in Bangladesh; and it is so rarely cold there that no heat is provided, even when the temperature dips into the 50s. The women were dressed in worn pale-pink, green, and yellow saris. Several of them were coughing. All of them were thin and looked old.

The exhibit consisted of a series of huge color photos of Yunus entering the hall in Oslo, giving his speech, and receiving the prize, as well as huge blown-up photos of the script of his Nobel lecture. This is creepy, I thought. Yunus is not dead. But it is as if he has already been enshrined and the vestal virgins are watching over the mausoleum.

When I left to go upstairs, the women turned out the lights and continued coughing and sweeping in the dark.

Awards Yunus Received Before the Nobel Peace Prize

Bangladesh: President's Award, 1978

Philippines: Ramon Magsaysay Award, 1984

Bangladesh: Central Bank Award, 1985

Bangladesh: Independence Day Award, 1987

Switzerland: Aga Khan Award for Architecture, 1989

United States: CARE's Humanitarian Award, 1993

Sri Lanka: Award for Science, 1993

Bangladesh: Rear Admiral M.A. Khan Memorial Gold Medal Award: 1993

United States: World Food Prize, 1994

United States: Pfeffer Peace Prize, 1994

Bangladesh: Dr Mohammad Ibrahim Memorial Gold Medal Award, 1994

Switzerland: Max Schmidheiny Foundation Freedom Prize, 1995

Bangladesh: Rotary Award, 1995

Venezuela & UNESCO: Simon Bolivar Prize, 1996

United States: Distinguished Alumnus Award of Vanderbilt University, 1996

United States: International Activist Award, 1997

Norway: Help for Self Help Prize, 1997

Italy: State of the World Forum, 1997

United Kingdom: One World Broadcasting Trust Media Award, 1998

Spain: The Prince of Asturias Award for Concord, 1998

Australia: Sydney Peace Prize, 1998

Japan: Ozaki (Gakudo) Award, 1998

India: Indira Gandhi Prize for Peace, Disarmament and Development, 1998

France: Juste of the Year Award, 1998

United States: Rotary Award for World Understanding, 1999

Italy: Golden Pegasus Award, 1999

Italy: Roma Award for Peace and Humanitarian Action, 1999

India: Rathindra Puraskar, 1998

Chapter One: **The Most Prestigious Prize in the World**

Switzerland: Omega Award for Excellence for Lifetime Achievement, 2000

Italy: Award of the Medal of the Presidency of the Italian Senate, 2000

Jordan: King Hussein Humanitarian Leadership Award, 2000

Bangladesh: IDEB Gold Medal Award, 2000

Italy: Artusi Prize, 2001

Japan: Grand Prize of the Fukuoka Asian Culture Prizes, 2001

Vietnam: Ho Chi Minh Award, 2001

Spain: International Cooperation Prize, 2001

Spain: Navarra International Aid Award, 2001

Gandhi International Peace Prize given by India to Grameen Bank

United Kingdom: World Technology Network Award, 2003

Sweden: Volvo Environment Prize, 2003

Colombia: National Merit Order Award, 2003

France: The Medal of the Painter Oswaldo Guayasamin Award, 2003

Spain: Telecinco Award, 2004

Italy: City of Orvieto award, 2004

United States: The Economist Innovation Award, 2004

United States: World Affairs Council Award, 2004

United States: Leadership in Social Entrepreneurship Award, 2004

Italy: Premio Galileo Special Prize for Peace, 2004

Japan: Nikkei Asia Prize, 2004

Spain: Golden Cross of the Civil Order of the Social Solidarity, 2005

Bangladesh: Bangladesh Computer Society Gold Medal, 2005

Italy: Prize ll Ponte, 2005

Spain: Foundation of Justice, 2005

United States: Harvard University, Neustadt Award, 2006

Netherlands: Franklin D. Roosevelt Freedom Award, 2006

Switzerland: ITU World Information Society Award, 2006

Korea: Seoul Peace Prize, 2006

Spain: Convivencia of Ceuta Award, 2006

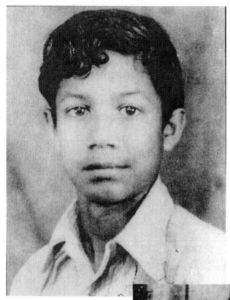

Yunus as a boy.

*Yunus (right) visits Europe and
the USA with the Boy Scouts.*

Chapter Two:
Childhood in Chittagong

I sat sipping tea in the cluttered office of Ibrahim, one of the younger brothers of Muhammad Yunus and a well-known physics professor. He was late for our meeting—stuck in traffic that was even worse than the usual nightmare that is taken for granted in Dhaka. It had taken me and my driver an hour and a half to inch our way from the Sheraton Hotel where I was staying to Ibrahim's office less than two miles away. As I sat waiting for him to arrive, I sneezed several times, and it occurred to me that I had succumbed to the cold that almost everyone I had met in Dhaka seemed to have. I had been interviewing people at the Grameen Bank for several days and I was discouraged about what I was hearing, which was familiar anecdotes and sound bites about Yunus. The staff were polite, but most of what they told me was shop-worn.

As I was thinking about my challenge to get people to open up, a younger, hippyish version of Yunus sprinted into the room. Ibrahim's rumpled, grayish black hair meandered down his back. He greeted me with a warm handshake followed by peals of laughter about nothing in particular. Ibrahim, I knew, was a professor of physics at Dhaka University and author of 37 books—clearly no slouch himself. Like Yunus, he is concerned about the poor. He founded the Center for Mass Education in Science (CMES), a not-for-profit organization, to take an understanding of science to rural youth in Bangladesh. I had learned reading his brochures that there were now branches of CMES sprinkled all over the country.

By the time an office boy had delivered a cup of steaming tea to Ibrahim, he was telling me one story after another about what it was like growing up with Yunus as his big brother. I was enchanted and relieved—here was the fresh material I was seeking. He explained that the family was traditional and middle class, but, of course, at that time, middle class meant poor. The family lived in the small port city of Chittagong in East Pakistan. His words tumbled out in a rapid stream.

Chittagong had been part of India and a British colony until Yunus was seven. After the partition of India in 1947, Chittagong was assigned to Pakistan. Finally, in 1971, it became part of the new country of Bangladesh. Though out of the way, the city had a long history of visitors from abroad, including many traders from Arabia and Burma. Its residents were mostly Bengali by ethnicity and culture and fiercely proud of their Bengal culture, with its long traditions of poetry and song. Yunus once told me that he had a hunch that perhaps the love of poetry and music came naturally to Bengalis because so many rivers flowed through the countryside. It was an interesting thought, but I didn't quite following his reasoning.

Ibrahim continued with a description of their house, which was located in the noisy, central part of the city. Their father's jewelry business was located on the street level, and the family lived on the upper levels in just five rooms. The family was large, with nine surviving children, seven boys and two girls. Salam, the oldest brother, and Yunus, the second boy, were buddies and always together. The next five children formed a pack, playing and hanging around together. Four of the boys slept in the same bed.

Ibrahim was like an engine just warming up, enjoying himself as he shifted to the subject of his parents. He talked so fast that a couple of time I had to ask him to repeat something as stories flew out of his mouth. He punctuated his comments with more laughter. "Our father, Dula Mia, barely finished high school, and he was anything but an intellectual. Still, he was determined that all his children would be well educated. What was most important to him was that all of us boys stay in school and that we all excel in our schoolwork. Unlike most businessmen in our city, he never tried to bring any of his children into his business. The children of most of his colleagues took up businesses as soon as they became teenagers. That was the usual tradition. So while many of our contemporaries were in business making money, since we had no money problems, we stayed in school, working hard at college and then university.

"Our father was caring but in a distant, not very intimate way. He was preoccupied with the business and did not pay close attention to us. So we did our own things, mostly. He also prayed a lot. Well, everybody who is a practicing Muslim prays a lot, because five times a day, that's a lot. Father gave us a lot of freedom and he did not really insist that we go to the mosque or anything. He would shout a lot about the bad things we were doing, not praying and not concentrating enough on the studies, but he did not insist on anything. And he would listen to us when we argued with him. It is not what we expect from traditional parents in Bangladesh."[1]

I was feeling better already as Ibrahim shared these personal recollections of the family. He went on to say that even though the children all did well in school, in many other ways they did the opposite of what their father wanted. For example, Yunus would be in his room, theoretically hard at work studying, but actually reading other kinds of books—histories, adventure stories, and novels. As soon as he heard their father's footsteps approaching, he would quickly grab the textbooks and look deeply engrossed in them. Ibrahim added, laughing gleefully once more, that he thought this was really "an open secret."

Like all devout Muslims, Ibrahim explained, their father believed that drawing images of people or any living creatures was evil. Yunus, however, had an interest in art from an early age. He found a teacher who taught him how to draw—and, of course, he neglected to mention these lessons to his father.

When Yunus and Salam, his older brother, were about 10 and 12, they were already fascinated by politics and international affairs. Every day they would go around the corner to a doctor's office and read all the magazines in the waiting room, including *Time* and *Newsweek,* cover to cover. They lifted money from their father's pockets for snacks and movies. Their father, preoccupied with his business, did not notice that the money was missing.

Ibrahim's voice softened as he shifted the topic to his mother, Sofia Khatun. He explained that she became mentally ill when Yunus was 10 and he was five, and that her mother and her sisters also had mental problems. She could be very violent, and she shouted all the time. It was scary for the children, but at times they made fun of her behavior and had signals to warn each other about her moods. Sometimes she would be coherent; at other times she would not even recognize her children.

Later that week, when I asked Yunus about his mother, he said that before she became sick she was the disciplinarian in the family, the one with the firmer hand. She helped their father with the finishing touches on pieces of jewelry and she had compassion for the poor, neighbors, and extended family. Although his mother herself was not at all formally educated, she read a lot and had a wonderful memory. She would tell stories from history, myths, and legends. Sometimes she would make up her own rhymes in the stories. "At the beginning," Yunus explained, "I didn't understand that something is wrong with her. I thought this is the ways she says things, maybe. It's strange to me, but maybe true. And she could be throwing things and not knowing what she was throwing. Since I was very close to her, I'd go and jump and snatch things from her hand so she couldn't throw them."[2]

Yunus added that his mother always remembered her five children who had died as babies. "She would say, 'This one would now be this old and she would be in grade seven.' To her, some were on this side, some on the other side, so she always had the full family."[3] While it was sad to lose so many children, he said, it was usual in the Chittagong of his youth. He said that his family was considered very fortunate to have nine children who survived.

Back to my interview with Ibrahim. I asked about what family life was like after their mother became sick. He told me that their father bathed the children himself and dressed them for school. He always had a couple of teenage boys as domestic help who assisted with the young children and who, according to Ibrahim, usually became part of the family. Their father calmly and with great patience took care of their mother for the 30 years until she died. And he always insisted that the children be respectful to her. When the sons were adults and any of them came home, before he even talked to them he would tell them to go say hello to their mother.

I changed the subject to ask Ibrahim about something that had been confusing me. Why was it that no one in the family had the same name as their father or mother? He explained that, by tradition, it was a matter of choice. Some families have family names while others, like their family, don't. Their father chose names from the Bible to go with Muhammad for the older boys – Muhammad Yunus (Jonah) and Muhammad Ibrahim (Abraham). Of course, he added laughingly, "Millions of Muslim boys have the name Muhammad."[4] For the younger boys their father chose Mogul and Indian names. Ibrahim added that the trend today is toward family names. Ibrahim has given Ibrahim as a family name to his two sons, as Yunus has given Yunus to his two daughters.

When I asked Ibrahim to describe what Yunus was like as a boy, he said that Yunus explored everything. He had the use of a neighbor's dark room and developed his own photographs. He and Salam organized a thriving stamp business at a nearby store when they were still very young. Yunus was interested in the arts: drawing, mapping, singing songs, performing. He played the harmonica very well, almost professionally. By the time he was 12, he had written a detective novel. When he sent a postcard, he always wrote an original poem on it.

Ibrahim leaned forward and said to me with a note of pride, "Yunus and I were very close. If someone had interviewed me when I was twelve and he was seventeen, I could have told them everything that Yunus was doing, every point he was worried about, every point where he took issues with others, and any problems he had with his group of friends."[5]

According to Ibrahim, Yunus became the center of gravity in the household and the leader of the siblings at an early age. The oldest, a sister, had been married as a teenager and left the family to live with her husband. Salam, who was two years older than Yunus, was more reserved than Yunus by temperament. Yunus always organized the children but at the same time encouraged all of the brothers and his younger sister to go their own ways rather than imposing his ideas on any of them. For example, Yunus helped Ibrahim pursue his interest in science even though he himself was much more interested in the arts. Soon Ibrahim had his own home laboratory, and by the time he was in high school he had started a science magazine.

Ibrahim launched into another story. When Yunus was 13, he was determined to get Ibrahim accepted

into his Boy Scout troop, despite the fact that he was
only eight, much younger than the required age. Already
a creative problem-solver, Yunus came up with a way
to make this happen. There was soon to be an event
celebrating a famous Pakistani poet. Yunus helped
Ibrahim learn several of his poems. This was difficult
because they were written in Urdu, not the boys' native
Bengali. Yunus also prepared a speech about the poet
and taught Ibrahim how to deliver it in a dramatic style.
At the event, everything went off according to plan.
Ibrahim gave the speech with the appropriate gestures
and recited the poems by heart. Since he was only eight,
he impressed everyone with his performance. And
because the Scout master depended on Yunus to keep
discipline, he agreed to Yunus's request for his little
brother to join the troop as a guest member.

As I left Ibrahim's office after almost two hours, I felt
energized and ebullient—clearly his good spirits were
contagious. And more important, Ibrahim had given me a
feel for the chemistry among the brothers and a sense of
the world that shaped Yunus as a youth.

When I met with Jahangir, another of Yunus's younger
brothers and the eighth in line of the children, he added
another family perspective. Taller than Yunus and movie-
star handsome, Jahangir, a well-known media personality,
hosts a television show on current events. He, like
Ibrahim and Yunus, lives in Dhaka, while all the other

siblings stayed in Chittagong. He described the youthful Yunus as a versatile genius. He recalled how Yunus adored movies and saw many of them over and over again. Whenever he came back from a movie, he would mesmerize the younger children with colorful renditions of the plot, with all its many twists and turns. These sessions inspired Jahangir's love of film and drew him towards the media and his future career.

When I sat with Yunus a few days after my talks with his brothers, he provided more details that deepened my understanding of him as a boy. He explained that, while the family constituted a rather laissez-faire environment, the schools in Chittagong had been anything but permissive. In the primary school, there were always about 40 boys in a class, and the emphasis was on memorizing and discipline. When Yunus was in the fifth grade, he received the highest score on the city's exam and won a scholarship to the Chittagong Collegiate School.

Several years later he was offered another scholarship, this time to study in England for "college"—what in the United States is still high school, the last two years before going on to a university. He turned down the scholarship to attend a local college. One of the college's attractions was its Boy Scout program. Besides, Yunus said, he didn't yet understand his own country. It is interesting to ponder what a difference in his development might have been made if he had he spent those formative years in Great Britain.

Yunus's scouting experiences were a major factor in shaping the man he would become: "The scout den became my hangout." Along with boys from other schools, he engaged in drills, games, artistic pursuits, discussions, hikes in the countryside, variety shows, and rallies. "During 'earnings week' we would raise money by hawking goods, polishing boots and working as tea stall boys. Aside from the fun scouting taught me to be compassionate, to develop an inner spirituality and to cherish my fellow human beings."[6]

When Yunus was 13, he was selected to go to a Boy Scout jamboree in Karachi, in West Pakistan. This required a train trip from Chittagong and East Pakistan across the whole of India, with stops along the way to see sights such as the Taj Mahal. The trip gave Yunus an opportunity to meet boys from all over his country. When he was 15, in 1955, he was one of the scouts from Pakistan chosen to attend the international jamboree in Canada. His father supported these trips, even though they cost money. He always said that it was good to go out and see the world. He himself had gone on the Hajj—the religious pilgrimage to Mecca in Saudi Arabia required of all Muslims—three times.

Yunus recalled his trip to Canada this way. "We were a group of 27 boys and three leaders. We traveled by air to London and then from there by ship, by luxury liner, for 15 days to New York. We were treated like dignitaries. We were met by the mayor of New York, and a picture of us appeared in the *New York Times*. On the way home, we decided to use the airfare money to buy three buses in Germany at the Volkswagen factory and to tour around Europe. Everything in the countryside was devastated because the war was barely over. Since there was no deadline about when we had to get back home, we would sit down with a map each morning and talk about where to go. Some would suggest going to go one place, while others would push for another direction. We could go anywhere. That freedom gave us an amazing chance to plan and learn about the historical sites. We traveled across Europe and the Middle East and then finally Pakistan and Chittagong. The whole trip took us six months. Six months of freedom. So that was an absolutely amazing, amazing experience for us. We met so many people, so many different ideas. We talked all the time and we had all the time in the world."[7]

When Yunus arrived home from Canada, he gave each of his six brothers a pair of blue jeans from America. This was more than just a gift; wearing jeans from the States, rather than the traditional dress, was a statement and began a cultural shift within the family. He had also learned some American slang that he taught his brothers, and he recounted long stories of his travels and many adventures during his six-month odyssey. So even though their house was small and their upbringing traditional, their home was also in some ways becoming global.

As he was growing up, Yunus had thought he would be a lawyer, because almost all of the important leaders in Pakistan were lawyers. But by the time he was in college, it occurred to him that the most important challenges were economic and concerned with the development of the country. At that point he changed his focus to economics and decided he would become a teacher. After completing his studies at the University of Dhaka in 1961, he took a job as an economics teacher back at the college he had attended in Chittagong and taught there for four years.

While a student at college, Yunus acted in plays and performed humorous skits for his fellow students. He and a friend developed quite a following, and a number of villages in the region around Chittagong invited them to put on shows. Yunus recalled how much he enjoyed seeing the audience laughing at what he was doing, and he even got paid small amounts of money for these performances.

One favorite act, which his audiences loved, was a monologue where he played a village woman, a kind of country bumpkin. Home after her first visit to a big city, she regaled the women in her village with her impressions. Even as a student, it seems, Yunus had an empathic understanding of how village women thought and felt and how they would react to a glimpse of the world beyond the confines of their homes.

On the side, while he was teaching, Yunus established a business that made boxes as well as printing cards, calendars, and books. Soon the business employed 100 people and was flourishing. Today it continues to prosper and is managed by his youngest brother. This early success—he was not yet 25—signaled to Yunus that he was gifted as an entrepreneur and that a career in business was clearly one of his options.

It's sometimes said that the apple doesn't fall far from the tree. In the case of Yunus, it seems at first glance that the apple fell quite a distance. By the time he was 25, the gulf between his parent's lifestyle and his own was already huge. Compared to his father, he was more secular, more educated, more worldly, with an astounding array of interests far beyond anything his father had experienced. He had spent six months in the United States and travelling across Europe while his mother knew nothing beyond the confines of her home. But at the same time he embraced many of the values of his family: he was disciplined, hard-working, and non-authoritarian. From his mother, he got his abilities as a storyteller and his gift with words.

How Yunus evolved is understandable when you look at the dynamics of family. His father was a businessman who valued education more than business and who in many ways gave free rein to his children. He encouraged his sons to turn their backs on the narrow path he had chosen for himself. His mother was unpredictable and mentally ill and, after Yunus was 10 years old, could not function as a parent. Without minute by minute supervision by the parents, Yunus had a chance to develop his varied interests—politics, international affairs, economics, history, storytelling, theater, photography, literature, and the arts. But he had also been cast, prematurely perhaps, into the role of leader in the family. With the illness of his mother, it is safe to say that Yunus did not get all the mothering and nurturing that he would have needed. And he missed the chance to lean on others as well as to be the responsible one. Typically, the parentified child over-functions and doesn't know how to ask for help.

Many facets of Yunus the man were evident by the time he was 25. As a boy, he had already shown his promise as an entrepreneur with his stamp business and in his early twenties with his packaging company. His talents as a performer were well honed. His leadership skills were apparent in every setting, whether in the family, at school, or in the Scouts. In some senses he was already a global citizen, having been exposed to a wide range of people and cultures on his travels. What had not yet manifested itself, however, was his vocational direction. He was a polymath looking for a mission, and some years would pass before he would find it.

Yunus on graduation day.

Chapter Three:
Yunus in the U.S.A.

Young women dressed in skimpy shorts and halter tops lounged on the grass on the campus of the University of Colorado at Boulder. What could be more shocking to a young Muslim man from the conservative city of Chittagong, Pakistan, where no nice girl would even think of showing her ankles? Yunus recalls the jolt he experienced when he arrived in the United States for his Fulbright in 1965. Casual encounters with women who were not part of his family just didn't happen back home. At his old college there, the few girls had been confined to the Women's Common Room when they were not in class. Later, when he was at Dhaka University, it had not been much different. The women sat apart from the men in every class and kept their eyes down, as was the custom.

After spending the summer in Colorado, Yunus went to Vanderbilt University in Nashville, Tennessee. He was excited about a chance to study development economics at an American university—although, when he got the word of this placement, he had never heard of Vanderbilt and had to consult a map to learn where Tennessee was located.

It was not just the role of women that was different in the United States, compared to Pakistan; the whole educational system was different. Yunus marveled when students interrupted lectures with questions and when they freely stated their own views. Most surprising of all, the professors usually welcomed their comments. Outside class he observed students and teachers mingling on the campus and chatting together. Back home, the difference in status between students and professors prevented any contact between them except in class.

At first Yunus found Vanderbilt disappointing. He was bored by his courses that were less advanced than those he had taken back home. There were no other students from Pakistan. Shy to begin with, he avoided talking to any of the women students. He remembers trying hard not to look at any of them. He was lonely, spending most of his time in his room watching television. His favorite shows were *60 Minutes, I Love Lucy,* and *Gilligan's Island.* To this day he loves TV. But now he insists he has no favorite programs and the TV is just background noise while he does work on his computer.

It was not until his second year at Vanderbilt, when Yunus took a statistics course with a brilliant Romanian mathematician and economist, Nicholas Georgescu-Roegen, that he became fully engaged with his academic work. Georgescu-Roegen was a different kind of teacher from any Yunus had known before—one who led the students gradually down the pathway of discovering independently the solutions to problems. Yunus recalled, "He went to the core of knowledge rather than just giving the technical details. Usually students ended up with Fs and Ds. I got an A. So people looked at me and said, 'My God, he got an A.' And he liked me, and I liked him."[1]

The following year Yunus took an economic theory class with Georgescu-Roegen that he found even more compelling than the statistics course he had taken the year before. And the year after that, Georgescu-Roegen invited him to be his teaching assistant. Yunus told me, "The most difficult thing, he made it simple."[2] Yunus came to believe that it was arrogance that prompts people to translate problems into more and more complicated formulations.[3] His work with Georgescu-Roegen provided him with the intellectual foundation that would underlie his thinking for the next 45 years. He had also acquired a bias toward action and a belief in experiential education. To this day, one of Yunus's signature lines in speeches is, "Things are never so complicated as they seem."[4] This idea annoys some of his audience; others find it intriguing and compelling.

The second half of the 1960s, when Yunus was studying in America, was the height of the Civil Rights movement. "Everything I read was about civil rights, what terrible things were happening in the South, how

the Ku Klux Klan was punishing people because they
are black, they are hanging them, they are burning them."
Yunus recalled, "I couldn't understand why people could
be so cruel to other people, just because they seem to
be another color. I was another color!"[5] And, in fact,
when Yunus had first arrived in Nashville he was not sure
whether or not he would be perceived as black and what
might happen to him if he were. His white friends told
him not to worry, but Tennessee was the south and he
remained uncomfortable as a person of color.

When Martin Luther King was assassinated in
Memphis in 1968, the blacks in Nashville were outraged.
Yunus and a friend drove to a black neighborhood to see
what was going on. The anger of the blacks in the streets
was terrifying, so Yunus and his friend made a hasty
retreat.

The late 1960s were also the years of widespread
protests against the war in Vietnam. Before coming to the
States, Yunus, like most university students in Chittagong,
had harbored negative feelings about America's role
in the war. He recalled, "We blamed the Americans for
causing all this trouble. They are the imperialists and
they are the people who were warmongers. They don't
understand anything but money. They want to fight wars
so they can make more money. They are the colonials."[6]
When he arrived at Vanderbilt, he quickly discovered
that that many students all over the United States also

opposed the war. He joined the protest efforts at Vanderbilt, marching in a number of anti-war rallies.

Yunus was astonished by the way some young people behaved. "This was the peak of the hippie, the flower children. We were hearing, 'If you are over 30, you are not to be trusted.' And the young people defied their parents and were out on their own, wearing rags and living like street people, with love-ins and so on. I saw a completely different world. I could not imagine these things could happen. But it was happening right in front of my eyes. And my friend on the right, my friend on the left, were the ones who were doing it. It was not happening somewhere else."[7]

Above all it was the personal freedom in the United States that had the biggest impact on Yunus. As long as you were not black, of course. "You're not scared of anybody. You enjoy yourself and nobody bothers about what you do, what you say. Nobody cares where you're from."[8] This was very different from the constricting culture of Chittagong, where young people did not dare to deviate from the old ways or to challenge them.

In his chilly office another January afternoon in 2010, Yunus, now a man of 70, talked about the dramatic changes in his views during his stay in America. He had come to believe that you don't have to respect all the views of older people. Of course, he had been a secret rebel back in Chittagong, but never openly defiant. Now he came to see that it was really all right to say what you believe. "If you persist in your values, if you hold onto your cause despite police atrocities and oppression, finally you would prevail."[9]

One day during Yunus's second year at Vanderbilt, a young woman named Vera Forostenko approached him in the library and introduced herself. He described her this way: "She was a very friendly person, she knew a lot of people, she could go to anybody and become friends very quickly, which I cannot do. I'm shy, withdrawn, distant. I don't volunteer myself to go and talk to new people."[10] Vera's family, immigrants from Russia, had settled in Trenton, New Jersey, after World War II. She spoke many languages and was getting her masters in Russian literature.

Vera completed her M.A. and left Vanderbilt in 1969, but by this time they had a close relationship. Letters flew back and forth. Yunus knew that in the future he would be returning home, and Vera pleaded to go with him. Despite his descriptions of daily life in Pakistan, she remained confident that she could adjust. Finally, Yunus agreed and they became engaged.

They were married in 1970 in New Jersey, in a simple civil ceremony unlike the huge, multi-day event that a typical wedding in Chittagong would have entailed. No one else from either of their families was there to celebrate. Yunus's family was upset because Vera was a foreigner, and Vera's family was also upset because Yunus was a foreigner.

After the wedding, they moved to Middle Tennessee State University, where Yunus was teaching. After a few months in Murfreesboro, a sleepy town out in the boondocks, they moved back to Nashville, which was livelier. By now he had received his PhD, having completed his dissertation, *Optimal Allocation of Multi-Purpose Reservoir Water—A Dynamic Programming Model*. This early work does not tempt even his most ardent fans.

While Yunus had been studying in the States, the tension back in Pakistan was heating up. From the time in 1947 when India was divided into a Hindu India and a Muslim Pakistan, realists had worried that this was an unworkable arrangement because Pakistan consisted of two segments, West Pakistan and East Pakistan, which were separated by a thousand miles. Still, hopes for the new country ran high, and for devout Muslims, like Yunus's father, the creation of Pakistan was a dream come true.

Yunus, who had been seven in 1947, recalls the excitement of the birth of the new country. His family spent the entire day making special foods for the celebration. At midnight, the whole family went up onto the roof of their house to watch as all the lights in Chittagong were extinguished and the city lay in total darkness for a moment. When they came back on a minute later, Pakistan had come into being.

While the two segments of Pakistan shared a common religion, most people in West Pakistan spoke Urdu while in East Pakistan, where Yunus grew up, everyone spoke Bengali. Although East Pakistan had the larger population, West Pakistan wielded more power; the capital was there, and West Pakistanis always were able to secure more of the top positions.

It was not long before serious problems erupted between the two segments. A turning point came when the central government decreed that Urdu would be the national language for both parts of the country and that schools in East Pakistan must use Urdu. This was an unacceptable insult to the East Pakistanis, who loved their language and their Bengal literature with its famed authors like Tagore. At that point, the movement for an independent East Pakistan, for a country to be called Bangladesh, gathered steam.

On March 17, 1971, Yunus was at home in Nashville listening to the news on the radio when he heard that East Pakistan was about to declare its independence. The West Pakistanis had sent troops and tanks into East Pakistan to quell the rebellion, and the East Pakistanis—now calling themselves Bangladeshis—were fighting back. For the Pakistanis it was a civil war; for the Bangladeshis it was a war of liberation.

Immediately Yunus leapt into action, calling a meeting for later that day of the five others from East Pakistan who lived in the Nashville area. Their mood was anxious, and they were uncertain about what to do. As Yunus remembers it, he announced right away to the group, "Bangladesh has declared its independence. Everybody has the right to choose. I declare my choice. My choice is Bangladesh."[11]

Once it was clear that all six of them were strongly in support of Bangladesh, Yunus put forth a plan of action. The six would form a Bangladeshi Citizens Committee to support the cause of the new country, and each of them would donate $1,000 to the effort. The Committee would focus its energies on meeting with the media— representatives from local TV stations and key editors— to garner support for an independent Bangladesh. When Yunus learned there was to be a pro-Bangladesh demonstration in Washington, D.C., a few days later, he decided to attend.

Once in Washington, Yunus met with the many others from East Pakistan who had come from around the United States to support the cause. The organization of the event was vague, however, and their group had not received a permit to hold a rally. Yunus feared the demonstration would be an embarrassing failure. Not being a person to sit by and let this happen, he rushed to a store, bought lots of colored paper, paint, and brushes, and started making festoons and signs. At the very last minute the permit arrived and they could proceed. It was a great relief to Yunus that many people attended the demonstration on the steps of the Capitol and the media gave it good coverage.

Meanwhile, not all the East Pakistanis in Washington came out in support of Bangladesh. Some of the diplomats at the Pakistani embassy argued that they could be more useful by keeping their jobs and not making any announcements about what their position was. Yunus not only disagreed with their stand, he again took matters into his own hands. If they would not plead the cause of Bangladesh to the international community in Washington, he would do it himself. He and a friend rushed from embassy to embassy, making the case for supporting Bangladesh to anyone who would talk to them.

At each embassy, however, they were asked if there was a government in Bangladesh—and they had to admit there wasn't any yet. Because the leader of the independence movement in Bangladesh had been arrested, it was not clear whether anyone was actually in charge. Yunus convinced the group of Bangladeshis gathered in Washington that perhaps they could be a catalyst to form a government. He volunteered to fly to Calcutta to bring together all the leaders from East Pakistan who had fled to India. He was disappointed when it was decided that someone else should go to Calcutta, and that he himself would follow only after a few days. Even more disappointing was the fact that the plan for a new government fizzled out completely.

Yunus's group, the Bangladesh League of America, as it came to call itself, shifted its focus to lobbying the U.S. government to stop giving military aid to Pakistan. And for Yunus it was time to go back to Nashville, his job, and his wife. But to this day he remembers those several weeks of political activity as intoxicating and transformative.

The way Yunus sprang into action just minutes after he heard the news of the events in Bangladesh demonstrated his leadership ability. He could think quickly and make decisions in the midst of uncertainty. He sensed that this was a defining moment for his new country; and although he was halfway around the world he wanted to be a player and a leader in the action, not just an observer. Since he had no one interpreting for him what was happening, no one guiding him, he had to rely on his judgment to figure out what to do.

As the war continued, back in Nashville Yunus centered his life around his work in support of the Bangladeshi cause. He created a communications center for the Bangladesh League of America in order to keep all the East Pakistanis living in the United States informed about what was happening. Of course, creating a list of all the East Pakistanis in the States was much harder in the pre-Internet world of 1971 than it would be today. Vera, who was strongly committed to the cause, worked tirelessly alongside him.

It was George Harrison, the Beatle, who brought the plight of Bangladesh into the awareness of many Americans with his Concert for Bangladesh that summer of 1971. The press, however, was generally negative about the independence of Bangladesh, and the U.S. government kept sending more military aid to Pakistan. President Nixon and Secretary of State Kissinger clearly supported Pakistan and refused to recognize the independence of Bangladesh. Kissinger commented "The place is, and always will be, a basket case." The words "basket case," with their dismissive pessimism, became an iconic epithet that stuck like glue and is remembered to this day. Years later, it came to light that one of the reasons Nixon and Kissinger supported Pakistan was that Pakistan was facilitating talks between China and the United States and the relationship to China was hugely important to Nixon.

That summer of 1971, as the bloody battles in Bangladesh dragged on, Yunus returned to Washington to help with lobbying efforts. He recalls that the Bangladeshis there were desperate to get across their message that the old two-part Pakistan was gone, finished. It was an agonizing time for him, as in Bangladesh it was his friends and relatives who were being killed. The group in Washington threw themselves into their work of changing the attitudes of key government officials. Using the technology of the day, Yunus and a former teacher, Muzammel Huq, created file cards for all the congressmen and senators and added key facts about their views and interests, so the group's pitches could be customized for each legislator. Later in the fall, Yunus organized teach-ins in support of Bangladesh at university campuses around the country.

By November, the situation looked dire for the Bangladeshis. As defeat seemed likely, India, motivated by its long-standing antipathy to Pakistan and its cultural ties to Bangladesh, sent in troops to aid the Bangladeshis. This turned the tide. The war ended on December 16, 1971, with the surrender of Pakistan. Some believe it was just in time, as the U.S. Navy's 7th Fleet was steaming towards Bangladesh—perhaps in order to aid the Pakistanis. More than one million Bangladeshis—some estimates run as high as three million—had died during the nine months of the war.

Yunus knew it was time to go home to Bangladesh. He was 31 years old. He had been in the United States from 1965 to 1972 and had experienced the tumultuous changes in society here—the successes of the Civil Rights movement, the shift in attitudes toward the war in Vietnam, and a general relaxation of social mores. He now knew that it was possible for dedicated young people, on fire with a cause, to transform their society. He had seen it happen.

While he was in the States, Yunus had learned a great deal about how to organize and manage. He had observed how government works and understood more clearly now what were the actual levers of change. He had developed his skills in using the media to influence public opinion and in managing the nuts and bolts of lobbying. He had experienced the grueling day-to-day work of making change happen. In short, Yunus had acquired the practical skills of a change agent.

He had also demonstrated his remarkable ability to bring people together, and to modify plans as circumstances unfolded. Never reluctant to take on a leadership role, he had exhibited his willingness to lead in the midst of confusion and uncertainty. Perhaps more important, he had shown his ambition to take on a grand role himself.

The cause of independence for Bangladesh had awakened the deepest passion in him. He had been roused to a new level of focused activity that made clear the personal powers he possessed to make things happen when he had a cause he believed in. In some sense, a new Yunus had been born along with the new country of Bangladesh.

Chapter Three: **Yunus in the U.S.A.**

Professor Yunus.

Chapter Four:
Bangladesh, "a Basket Case"

There were no tourists in Bangladesh when I first went there in 1993. When I returned in 2010, there were still no tourists. A comment I overheard in the dining room of the Dhaka Sheraton captures why: "Bangladesh sure is a helluva difficult place to visit." On my most recent trip, when I tried to call my friend Anish Barua, I found the number didn't work. It took me a couple of days to realize that another digit had been added to all phone numbers since my last visit. Since there are no telephone books in Bangladesh and no information service, I was stymied. The list of day-to-day difficulties I encountered over my many trips is long: traffic jams, pollution, filth, extreme heat, streets without names, and maps without streets. But the electricity worked most days. And, of course, these inconveniences were minor compared to what those living in Bangladesh face on a regular basis.

In 1993, my first trip to Bangladesh, I arrived dazed from my 28-hour flight from Boston to Dhaka via London, Bahrain, and New Delhi. My fellow traveler and I stumbled into the steamy, dark, warehouse-like airport that was crowded with thousands of men (and a handful of women) pushing, shoving, and yelling. I smelled old sweat, cigarette smoke, and mold. The noise was excruciating. The suitcases came down a make-shift slide by ones and twos. After two long hours of anxious waiting, I felt intense relief when I finally caught sight of my bag. And then, as suddenly as a genie, a man with a sign saying UNICEF materialized out of nowhere to rescue us from the chaos. He whisked us away to an air-conditioned van and the more comfortable world of foreign consultants.

As we drove toward the center of Dhaka and the offices of UNICEF, the city on either side of the road pulsed with morning activities. Peering out the window, I saw women carrying loads on their heads and babies on their backs, emaciated goats being hurried along down the highway, and scrawny men on bikes pedaling furiously with loads of scrap metal on their backs. There were stalls where people were buying tea and open hovels where families huddled around small fires eating their breakfast. I had heard the pollution was terrible, but was still shocked by the greenish-gray cloud that hovered over the highway.

When Yunus and Vera arrived in Bangladesh in June, 1972, the scene was even more distressing. The whole country lay in ruins. Nothing worked. Institutions had fallen apart. There was no infrastructure. There was no government in action. The war had left a million people dead. Pakistani soldiers had slaughtered many intellectuals, murdered innocent people, and raped thousands of women. The atrocities committed by the Pakistanis left a legacy of bitterness that would not easily heal. Ten million people—mainly Hindus—had fled to India as refugees. They had been civil servants, the intelligentsia, the middle class—the kinds of people that were desperately needed to rebuild the country.

Yunus had always planned to return to Bangladesh, and during the months of the war he became increasingly uneasy remaining in America. "I felt like I was in prison," he recalled. "[Bangladesh] is where I live. That's where my life is, so that's where I should be, no matter how difficult it is. ... So when the war was over, this was the right time. And my wife knew that, so she packed up and we came. And we had no idea what I'd be doing."[1]

As Yunus took stock of his new country, the realities of its condition and resources were sobering. "Suddenly a province had become a country and we had to develop a system of governance. Now we were not looking to Islamabad, to wherever the big guys made decisions and we followed their instructions. We had to do it ourselves."[2] He remembered his frustration that there was no direction, no cohesion, no solidarity of the country as a whole. At the same time, he was euphoric, because Bangladesh was independent and free and it was a time of great hope. "But people were afraid the government was becoming more and more repressive. Everybody was suspecting everybody else. People were worried that there was some kind of conspiracy."[3] In fact, the People's Republic of Bangladesh was very unstable, the plots were real, and euphoria was short-lived.

Not only had Bangladesh been devastated by the war, but its geography created a host of difficulties for the new nation. Now it was a small country, roughly the size of the state of Wisconsin. Its 70 million people made it the most densely populated country in the world, and it had few natural resources besides water and soil. There was almost no stone in the country, and since only a small part of the land was forested, there were few materials available for construction.

Much of the country lay dangerously low, no more than 10 feet above sea level. Each year when the huge rivers, the Ganges and the Jamuna, flooded, they delivered new fertile soil for farming across the large delta that was Bangladesh. But this also meant that vast areas of the country were under water from mid-June through October—when the rains were relentless. The rainy season also brought diseases like typhoid and cholera. Other kinds of natural calamities—tornados, monsoons, tidal waves, droughts, and cyclones—battered Bangladesh with heart-breaking frequency. In 1970, just two years before Yunus returned to Bangladesh, more than 300,000 people had been killed by a cyclone.

Chapter Four: **Bangladesh, a "Basket Case"**

Bangladesh was one of the poorest countries on the planet. In 1972, more than half the people lived in poverty. Being poor meant children suffered from malnutrition and their growth was stunted. Being poor meant that the family lived on less than a dollar a day and sickness in the family could wipe out any savings. About 40 percent of the families in the country owned less than half an acre of land, which could not provide enough food for them. Child labor was taken for granted, and children who were poor almost never attended school.

For women, especially in the villages, life was harsh. In 1972, the average woman had had more than six pregnancies, and both maternal and infant mortality rates were among the highest in the world. It was the grandmothers and the aunts who delivered babies, as there were no medical facilities for women and almost no trained midwives. While many women died in childbirth, many children died of cholera, other diarrheal diseases, tuberculosis, and malaria. It was the custom for girls and women to eat after the men had finished their meal, and often this meant that the women went without. Bangladesh was one of the few countries in the world where women's life expectancy was less than men's.

When a girl child was born, there was no celebration. A girl baby in Bangladesh in 1972 was a burden—another mouth to feed and a cost to marry off. Almost at birth, the family started planning how to accumulate a bit of savings for the dowry they would need to give the bridegroom. Girls married young—usually by 16 and often as early as 10.

So this is what Yunus and Vera faced on their return to Bangladesh: a government that barely functioned, a country with few resources, and a population that was desperately poor. A former teacher of Yunus's, Nural Islam, who worked at the Planning Commission, persuaded him to accept a government job there. Yunus would have the opportunity to help design the new country—an exciting prospect—and he was given an impressive title: Deputy Chief of the General Economics Division.

For the first several weeks, Yunus appeared at his desk and sat all day waiting for work. Islam, his boss, told him to be patient; soon there would be more than enough work. Three months passed and he was still spending his days reading the newspapers. Frantic to address some of the challenges the country faced, Yunus wrote a letter of resignation, left it on his desk, and walked out.

Nural Islam caught up with Yunus a few weeks later. As Yunus remembered it, Islam told him that he couldn't just quit his job and that no one would hire him if he left the government with a bad record. To Yunus, this seemed preposterous, and he refused to go back. He was confident that he could find a job.

This negative experience in government service shaped Yunus's views about government for his entire life. He still sees governments as inefficient, bureaucratic, and—in the case of Bangladesh—usually corrupt and not to be trusted. He became convinced that to get anything done, he needed to look to the private sector.

Finding no suitable position at the University of Dhaka, his alma mater, Yunus went back home to Chittagong, where he was soon recruited to become the head of the Economics Department at the new Chittagong University. In 1972, many of the students were soldiers returning from the battleground. Some still carried their revolvers. These veterans felt they should be given their degrees without having to take exams. Yunus remembered, "So we were starting from there to bring discipline, to bring students into the classroom to take exams."[4] Gradually the students settled into their old routines.

Yunus had arrived at the university driving a white Volkswagen Beetle and sporting long hair and bell-bottomed pants. He looked totally different from all the other professors. H.I. Latifee, a colleague in the economics department, who still works with Yunus as head of the Grameen Trust, told me about his first impressions of Yunus. "He was smart, very friendly, charming, and he was a man who meant business."[5] Students flocked to his classes and afterward trailed behind him, eager for a word with their professor.

I finally did connect with my friend Anish (I got his phone number from UNICEF), and he remembered to this day the impression that Yunus had made on the campus. "We all heard that an American-trained professor with a Russian wife had arrived. I remember him saying that economics is a subject that needs to be felt, not just read. Also that you may get a very good job but don't get bogged down with the job. Do something so people can be benefited."[6]

As head of the economics department, Yunus was given a spacious office, while all the other 12 faculty members in the department shared a tiny one. Immediately, he decided to swap offices. Most of his colleagues thought giving up a perk that went with his position was inappropriate and foolish, while he was dumbfounded by their resistance to what seemed to him a common sense move. Already it was clear that his ideas and actions were going to upset some people; and it was clear that he was not afraid to go against custom and convention.

Yunus was eager to introduce his students to action-research, the learning-by-doing technique that had impressed him so much at Vanderbilt. A second goal was to deepen their understanding of why poverty was so endemic in Bangladesh. He was particularly concerned about the huge and growing number of landless poor people. With a grant from the Ford Foundation to support his work, Yunus established the Rural Studies Program, to learn more about the causes of poverty. The village of Jobra lay between the university campus and the city of Chittagong, where most of the students lived, and was thus a very convenient site for his students' field work.

One of his early projects entailed sending students out to interview 350 of the landless people in Jobra to learn about when and how they had lost their land. They discovered that most families had lost their land in the last 20 years. A family with a bit of land would run into a problem—an illness, a death, or a poor crop. Then they would have to borrow money for medicine, or for food, and soon they could not make the required repayments. Before long they would be forced to sell their land.

As part of the Rural Studies Program, some of his students ran an immunizations program in the village while others taught science to children. Still others, standing knee-deep in mud, helped farmers transplant their rice seedlings. Education at a Bangladeshi university had never been like this! For some, this kind of manual labor did not seem like a proper activity for university students, and they soon drifted away from the program. But other students were eager to work with Yunus.

With Latifee at his side, Yunus began to focus his efforts on helping the farmers in Jobra increase their food production. The two realized that if the farmers could irrigate their land during the dry winter season, a whole additional rice crop would be possible. Yunus learned about a high-yielding variety of rice that was grown in the Philippines and convinced the farmers in Jobra to try it. He observed that the village tubewell, a machine that could be used to capture underground water and irrigate the fields, was no longer in use. In fact, he found out that almost half of the tubewells in Bangladesh were no longer operating.

Latifee, a compact, hardy-looking man in his early seventies, told me in an interview about Yunus's early attempts to help the farmers of Jobra. "I was there from day one,"[7] Latifee said with pride as we sat in his unheated office on a cold day in January. He was bundled in a black quilted parka with a tan scarf around his neck. "We tried to understand what was going on and why no one used the well. We came to see there were conflicts, confusion, and misunderstandings and we discovered it was a management problem."[8] They finally were able to get the Jobra tubewell working again, but as harvest time approached, the farmers ran out of money for fuel, and Yunus had to bail them out with his own funds.

The next year Yunus came up with a new program to help the farmers of Jobra, which he called the New Era Three Share Plan. He and his students would manage the well, and they would pay for the fuel, the fertilizer, the insecticide, and the seeds. For this, they would be entitled to one-third of the yield. The farmers and the landowners would each take a third as well. Knowing that cooperation was difficult, he brought the farmers together for meetings and listened to their ideas about how best to get the work done. As the weeks passed and the fields turned emerald green, the farmers were thrilled. Their yield was double the national average. In the end, however, the farmers took more than their share of the rice and Yunus, who was clearly too trusting, was once again left with a debt to the bank. [9]

The next year Yunus refused to manage the program, although he did help the villagers to get a loan so they could continue to irrigate. He believed that the farmers needed to develop their own capacity to run the well and learn how to cooperate. The following year, the government took over the concept of the Three Share model and sponsored a series of programs. However, all the programs failed. Yunus was certain that this happened because the government did not include the villagers in any of the decision-making. It is ironic that, in spite of these failures, the government presented Yunus with a President's Award for his Three Share Plan.

And then in 1974, famine ravaged Bangladesh. Yunus remembers it this way. "In the beginning you don't notice it. You see skinny people lying down, sitting around, and children like old people, old people like children. ... And every morning, you hear that five dead bodies were recovered. And every day you see that this number is increasing. The people now are not violent, they are very quiet. Gradually you see this is serious. ... People had no clothes left, and people were selling off their children to survive."[10]

The government under the leadership of Sheikh Mujib, however, insisted that all the talk of famine was merely propaganda, and that people were just sick with diarrheal disease. They believed that for a shaky new government to admit there was a famine could be catastrophic. Yunus was upset by this denial; he wanted the situation confronted.

He figured that if he could convince the vice-chancellor of his university, a well-known writer named Abul Fazel, to sign a statement announcing that the country was experiencing a famine, it might get the government to face up to the situation. Yunus asked Fazel to write the statement, but Fazel insisted that Yunus write it. But then Fazel signed the statement without changing a word. Since the respected vice-chancellor had signed, the rest of the faculty followed suit. The next day, headlines in all the major newspapers in Bangladesh announced that the faculty of Chittagong University had signed a statement declaring that the country was experiencing a famine and asking the government to take action.

Chapter Four: **Bangladesh, a "Basket Case"**

Everybody wondered what the government would do about this. Very soon, the government declared a state of emergency, but because of the widespread corruption, none of their attempts to deal with the famine were effective. In August of 1975, members of the military who were dissatisfied with the present regime staged a coup and assassinated the leader, Sheikh Mujib, and most of his family. One daughter, Hasina, who just happened to be out of the country, survived, and she would play a decisive role in Yunus's life 35 years later.

Yunus had leapt into action on the national stage. He had been successful in shattering the government's conspiracy of silence about the famine and in alerting the whole nation to its plight. This was an amazing achievement for any one person, let alone a youthful professor.

But as the famine continued and the situation became more horrific, Latifee remembers Yunus saying to him, "I love teaching, but we can do something more."[11] In fact, Yunus came to believe that the economics he was teaching was all fairy tales that did nothing to address the plight of Bangladesh. He said, "Unless we do something, these made-up stories will not solve the problem. ... I don't know what to do. But one thing I know. I can be useful to somebody as a person, not an economist. That's useless. It doesn't help. As a person I can do something. Right here in this village. ... As a human being, I can be useful to one person, at least one person. So that was my theory."[12]

By 1975, Yunus had tried a number of ways to be of use in the village of Jobra—teaching, researching, improving the yield of the rice crop, and developing the Three Share Plan. He had experienced some successes and some failures. None of his projects had brought about fundamental change in the economic system or done anything significant to diminish the level of poverty.

He felt discouraged; he did not know where or how to use his tremendous life energy. To be so underutilized was incredibly painful. He could not know at this time that within months he would have his eureka moment and discover his mission.

Yunus in the early days of the Grameen Project.

Chapter Five:
Accidental Banker

One spring day in 1976, Sufiya Khatun was squatting in front of her house weaving a bamboo stool as two well-dressed men strolled through the village of Jobra. They paused right in front of her, so she lowered her eyes. One of them addressed her in a soft voice and asked her name. She could hardly speak. But as the men continued talking, asking her about her weaving and her work, she gradually found her voice. She explained that each day she had to borrow five takas (about 15 cents) from a trader to purchase the materials she needed to make the stools she sold for a living. In return for the loan, at the end of the day she had to sell back to the trader all the stools she had finished that day. He paid her so little that she made only about two pennies a day in profit—barely enough to survive. Sufiya was a widow with two children: five others had died. She felt trapped by her situation and could see no way to get out.

Yunus and his colleague Latifee were disturbed as they reflected on what Sufiya had told them. It seemed incredible that she could not manage to scrape together the tiny sum of five takas that it would take to get out of debt. They were disgusted by the system of bonded labor that left people like her in such dire circumstances; she seemed to be actually living in a kind of slavery. He wondered how many others in the village were working under similar arrangements and asked one of his students, Maimuna Begum, to canvass the village to find out.

A few days later Maimuna reported back to Yunus that she had found 42 people in Jobra who, like Sufiya, were living in the vicious cycle of a small debt they could never manage to pay. Their total debt amounted to 856 takas, or about $27. Yunus was stunned. He explained to me later how he had felt. "This was a big problem. This was something never taught in the classroom. In economics, there's no chapter called money lending. There's no chapter called loan sharks. And this is real, right here, in front of our noses. We teach economics and we don't know anything about it."[1]

During the next few days, Yunus kept turning over in his mind the question of why so many people had to suffer so much for such small amounts of money. The answer came to him in a flash. "There's such an easy way to solve it. That was what excited me, the simplicity of the solution. The idea is, if I give this money to all these people, they can return the money to the loan sharks and they'll be free. ... With $27, you have left this problem forever for these 42 people."[2] They could pay Yunus back whenever they were able.

He reached into his pocket and gave 856 takas to Maimuna to loan to the 42 villagers. He didn't ask for any interest or any collateral, but he did arrange for them to make daily payments to him at a local tea stall. He was focused on making it possible for them to pay back the loan sharks so that in the future they would be able to sell their products for much higher prices.

He was astounded by the impact of his $27. "They were so excited. I couldn't even imagine that this little money could bring so much excitement in their lives. Then it hit me. I said, if you can make so many people so happy with such a small amount of money, why shouldn't I do more of it?"[3]

Now Yunus was aware, in a way he had never been before, of how desperately people in the villages needed credit and how expensive it was for them to get it. He was even more amazed when the 42 villagers paid back, day by day, all the money they had borrowed from him. It dawned on him that there was no need for collateral from the poor; it appeared that they would pay their debts without it. With that flash of insight, he had found his mission. For the next 30 years he would focus his energies on trying to get small loans into the hands of more and more poor people.

Of course, he realized at the same time that he couldn't fund all the poor people even in a single village from his own pocket. He was also well aware that at that time no bank in the country provided any financial services to the poor. But he hoped that, once he reported to the bankers about his experiences in Jobra, some of them would understand, as he did, that lending to the poor was reasonable. If banks began to lend money to the poor, everything might change for them.

The very next day, as Yunus remembers it, he went to see the local manager of the Janata Bank, a man who had worked with him on the Three Share Project. Yunus told his story, made his pitch, and immediately hit a wall. The manager explained all the reasons why loans to the poor were out of the question. First, the forms for loans were costly, and the interest from such small loans would not even begin to cover the cost of the paperwork. Second, since poor people were illiterate, they couldn't even read the applications for a loan or fill out the forms. Finally, of course, the major obstacle preventing the bank from lending to the poor was the fact that they had no collateral. Yunus explained how his borrowers had paid back their loans without having given any collateral. He kept asking himself, why does there have to be collateral?

"That is our bank rule," the manager replied. [4] After a long back and forth conversation, the manager announced that his branch didn't give loans anyway. Only the head office, in Chittagong, gave loans.

So Yunus went to Chittagong to plead his case with the regional manager of the Janata Bank, R. A. Howlader, who turned out to be quite sympathetic to him and his ideas. Howlader explained that, although the lack of collateral was the main reason the bank could not lend money to the poor, if a wealthy person would guarantee the loans, then it might be possible. Yunus saw the pitfall in this idea: A wealthy person might easily take advantage of the poor just the way the loan sharks and traders had been doing for centuries. He finally concluded that the only safe way for the bank to start lending to the poor was if he himself volunteered to be the guarantor. Howlader knew that Yunus was a respected professor at the Chittagong University and that his father was a businessman who had resources. Yunus assured him that he was seeking only 10,000 takas, about $300, for his project. They agreed to move ahead and made a deal.

Yunus was disturbed by this exchange. It made him angry that he could be trusted with a loan while none of the villagers in Jobra were seen as credit worthy. If the bank would trust him, why wouldn't they trust the poor? So after the deal was done, he announced to Howlader that if any of the villagers defaulted on their loans, even though he was the guarantor, he would not pay them. He said he was certain that none of them would default, but if they did, he wouldn't pay. Let the bank take him to court! In reality, he could be fairly confident that the bank wouldn't take the highly respected Professor Yunus to court or pursue legal action for a mere $300.

Latifee remembers this story and saw Yunus's way of handling the situation as bold and principled. However, to Howlader, Yunus must have seemed ungrateful and like a loose cannon. Yunus recalls that he wanted to be the "stick in the wheel." He was out to change the whole system, and now he was beginning to see how he could do it. But it was incidents like this one that led numbers of people to conclude that Yunus was arrogant, unpredictable, and difficult to work with.

Even though a deal had been struck, it took another six months, until January 3, 1977, to get over all the bureaucratic hurdles required to disburse 16,000 takas, about $500, to seven people in Jobra, with Yunus co-signing each loan. At that point, he had already gone beyond the $300 limit to which he had agreed, making it quite clear that he was determined to expand his loaning operations no matter what he had agreed to earlier.

With their new capital, several of the seven of those who got loans purchased rickshaws, and several others bought cows. Sufiya, who got the very first loan, gave up making bamboo stools. With this loan of 50 takas, she bought some cheap jewelry and candy and became a peddler.

Yunus formed an organization called the Jobra Landless Association to make more loans to people in the village. He had no staff, no building, no processes, and no procedures. He recalls, moreover, that he had no idea where all this would lead. He certainly had no intention of starting a bank. His goal was merely to get capital into the hands of as many as possible of the poor villagers who wanted to grow their small businesses or start new ones. Having all his loans go to small businesses seemed like the best way to improve lives and alleviate poverty. He was thrilled, but not surprised, when the next group of villagers who received loans behaved exactly as he had predicted: They repaid their loans.

At this time, when Yunus was making his first loans to the poor, Vera became pregnant. For some time it had been evident to many of the staff at the Bank that she seemed unhappy living in Bangladesh. Their house out by the university was remote from the city, and she had not found a role for herself. In March, 1977, she gave birth to a daughter whom she and Yunus named Monica. They chose the name because it would work well in both the United States and Bangladesh.

When Monica was a few months old, Vera decided that Bangladesh was not a suitable place to bring up her child. In July, she returned with the baby to New Jersey, where her family lived. Yunus was devastated. Vera urged him to emigrate to the States and join her and the baby. He loved Vera and wanted to be with his daughter, yet he couldn't leave, couldn't give up his work in Bangladesh now that he was clear on his direction.

He did not want the marriage to end. But as the months passed and it was evident that Vera and he were going to be living on opposite sides of the world, divorce seemed necessary. After the divorce, Vera made things even more difficult for Yunus by refusing to let Monica go to Bangladesh to visit.

Whenever I was interviewing any of the old-timers at the Grameen Bank who had been with Yunus since Jobra, and I asked about Vera and her departure, I met a stone wall of resistance. After a comment about Yunus's huge personal sacrifice, they would give me a stern look that said, "Don't ask more about this." One woman, after I mentioned the divorce, silently shook her head and made gestures with her hands indicating for me to stop. I was recording the interview and realized that she didn't even want her "no comment" to be on the record.

Despite the turmoil in his life, Yunus worked hard that year to provide credit to more villagers. At the same time, he observed that the Janata Bank seemed to be deliberately putting up roadblocks by slowing down the lending process. Each loan proposal had to be sent to Dhaka for approval, and Yunus had to sign every document. In 1977 he went to the United States for three months as part of the Bangladesh delegation to the United Nations. Even then, the Bank insisted he be the one to sign all the paperwork. Each application was sent by airmail to him in New York, he would sign it, and then he would mail it back to Bangladesh.

In all of 1977, held back by administrative red tape, the Janata Bank made loans to only 65 people, although hundreds of others were waiting. At that point, Yunus realized he needed to find another bank that would be more cooperative.

He called A. M. Anisuzzaman, the managing director of the Krishni (Agriculture) Bank in Dhaka, and proposed that the Krishni Bank set up a special branch to lend money to the poor, a branch that would be under Yunus's own direction. He would set the terms and create the procedures. It would be an experiment to see whether lending to the poor was really viable. Anisuzzaman was willing to try out the concept, but his colleagues and the government-appointed board of directors were less enthusiastic. Finally, as a compromise, they gave Yunus a small outpost branch that was still formally under the direction of Krishni, but which, in reality, Yunus could manage as he wished.

The results were impressive. In the first two months, Yunus was able to make more loans than in the 15 months working with the Janata Bank. By September, 1978, 398 people had taken out small loans that amounted to almost half a million takas or about $15,000. Their repayment rate was an astonishing 98 percent, far higher than the 60 percent rates that were typical for commercial and government banks.

Yunus consulted with villagers to learn their views about how the loan process should be set up. He firmly believed that these landless poor people would know what would work for them and what would not. The villagers came up with the idea of forming support groups made up of borrowers in the same business, such as rickshaw pullers, bamboo-stool makers, and people raising cows. He liked the idea and implemented it right away.

The groups were naturally of quite different sizes, some large and others small. In many cases, members of the same group were in the same family; in other cases, they were competitors, which made cooperation difficult. Over time, Yunus discovered that smaller groups of five unrelated people who worked in different kinds of enterprises worked better than the original concept. At first he had thought it made sense for borrowers to make repayments on a daily basis, but the many tiny transactions were a burden to record, and he soon switched over to weekly repayments.

Yunus knew intuitively that he couldn't just replicate the way banks in Bangladesh did business. He was learning by trial and error how to work with borrowers who were poor, and he was developing his modus operandi step by step. He still did not think of himself as a banker—he was a professor running an experimental project.

Yunus was not the first person in the world to provide loans to the poor, and he was well aware of that. In the 1960s, Dr. Akter Hameed Khan had pioneered a cooperative program in East Pakistan that provided small amounts of credit to farmers. Yunus was an admirer of Khan and knew all about his work, but he disagreed violently with his model because it was mandatory and because it involved the government. An organization named Accion had been lending small amounts of money to poor people in Venezuela since the 1960s and in Brazil since 1973. In fact, the history of providing financial services to the poor goes much further back than the 1960s. Burial clubs in ancient Greece and Rome, medieval guilds, Irish loan societies, credit cooperatives in Germany, and cooperative savings and loan associations in Britain are all examples of organizations that lent money to the poor.

Yet it is the story of how Yunus lent $27 to 42 poor people in Jobra that has become legendary. He tells it in almost every speech he gives, and it has been retold in literally hundreds of articles about him and about microcredit. Sometimes Jobra is understood as the moment when microcredit or small loans to the poor came into being for the first time in history. This is of course a misunderstanding. Yunus has never claimed to have invented the idea of providing small loans to poor people or to have been the first to do it. He never called himself the father of microcredit, though others persist in referring to him that way. But his lending *process* was different from the way all banks he knew about operated. He had developed a new model that worked for the poor.

What also happened at Jobra is that Yunus identified his mission and his life's work. He had been struggling to find a way to be useful to his country. Now he realized that small loans could permanently improve the lives of the poor. He saw glimmerings of how he could make a significant difference and how he could affect the system that kept the poor in Bangladesh trapped in lives of poverty.

There is still more that is significant about Jobra. Yunus was able to turn the story of Jobra and how he became an accidental banker into a compelling narrative. That story—the eureka moment when everything changed—is still exciting. Skeptics wonder whether it all happened exactly the way Yunus tells it in his autobiography, *Banker to the Poor*. But that is not the point. Critics say it was self-promotion. I agree; he certainly has used the Jobra story to promote his work and his new way of lending to the poor. Yunus's story is how he has leveraged change. What is there to criticize about that?

Most important, for decades people have been profoundly moved by the story of Jobra. Hearing Yunus tell it has changed their lives. They have headed for Bangladesh, abandoned their former careers, found new

Woman making baskets in front of her home.

A typical center in the countryside – just one room.

Chapter Six:

Upside Down Banking

"Good women don't go from house to house,"
complained Nurjahan, a young woman in her early 20s,
after her first few days on the job at the Grameen Bank
Project in October, 1977. "I am feeling uncomfortable,"
she told Yunus.[1] Having just finished her master's degree,
Nurjahan had sought a position appropriate to her
level of education. She now realized that her job with
Grameen required her to spend most of her days walking
from one village to another, explaining to poor women
why they should take out a loan. It was the monsoon
season and it was raining night and day. The paths to
the villages were deep with mud, and from time to time
someone would shout a nasty comment to her as she
passed by. She had led her mother to believe that she
had a desk job.

Yunus asked Nurjahan to hold off for at least two
weeks before making any decision about quitting. He
then gave her a special assignment—to go to Jobra to
interview one of his poorest borrowers, a woman named
Ammajan. He told Nurjahan to take all the time she
needed to get a complete picture of Ammajan's life and
then to write up what she had learned in a case study.

He cautioned her not to disturb the village woman's daily routine but to question her only at moments when she was free to talk.[2]

Over their seven days together, Nurjahan observed the realities of Ammajan's life, learned about her history, and came to see how she experienced her world. Each day Nurjahan would prepare a new list of questions, and at night she would write up what she had learned. Gradually Ammajan began to talk freely. She told Nurjahan that her first husband had beaten her for years and described how she managed to survive when her second husband abandoned her. She shared her sadness at the deaths of five of her six children and what it was like when she was forced to become a beggar. And she explained how her life got better when she got a loan from the Grameen Bank. She could go to the bazaar and buy small items and then come back to Jobra and sell them.

"This case study changed me," Nurjahan explained to me more than 30 years later in a 2010 interview.[3] It taught her what it really was like to be poor and to grasp what Yunus was trying to accomplish when he talked about lifting people out of poverty. She decided to stay on at the Grameen Bank Project at least for a while, despite the difficulties. That was 1977.

In 2010, when I was ushered into Nurjahan's office on the eleventh floor of the Grameen Bank, she was sitting at her desk talking on one of the two phones in front of her. A small woman in her late 50s, she was wearing a black head scarf that covered her hair and a baggy black sweater over her dark sari. She looked more like a nun to me than an executive of a major bank. Her speech, however, had the ring of authority. Her English was serviceable if not fluent, and the fact that the tenses of her verbs floated around did not prevent her from plowing briskly ahead in conversation.

Nurjahan described how difficult it had been for village women in the early days of Grameen. The traditions of purdah—practices that protected Muslim women's modesty and purity—had been still alive and well in Jobra and the surrounding villages. A modest woman never left her home and never showed her face to any man outside the family. Some women, like Nurjahan's mother, carried these practices of purdah to such an extreme that, in addition to wearing a sari which successfully blurred the outlines of the body with its many yards of material, they always wore socks and gloves to shield their hands and feet from view. And this in a climate where it can hover at 115 degrees for weeks. Other women, especially poor women who needed to work outside the home, interpreted the restrictions of purdah less strictly.

Most village women, Nurjahan told me, were malnourished, and their children were malnourished as well. Sometimes families had food for only one meal a day. Since there were no toilets and few outhouses in the countryside, women would sneak out in the dark to relieve themselves behind nearby bushes. Typically women kept nearly silent in the home; when they did speak, they spoke softly, their eyes cast down. Wife beating was common, a taken-for-granted part of marriage. In the 1970s, people in the villages were not only ignorant but also superstitious. For example, most women believed that an amulet around the neck was the best way to keep a baby healthy.

Yunus had observed that women who borrowed from his Grameen Bank Project used their money to improve their families' lives, while men tended to spend their loan money on non-essentials like snacks or a new shirt. He realized how much more impact his loans would have if he focused on lending to women. He said, "I wanted to be sure that half the borrowers in my program were women… And then I got to the women, and women said 'No, not to me, you give it [the loan] to my husband,' or 'I never touch money. I don't want to get involved with this. I don't want to create a problem for my family.'"[4]

He recalled to me how he explained to his staff about the women's resistance. "It's not their voice. It is the voice of history … she doesn't want to get into trouble … she's protecting herself. I said it will take a lot of time and a lot of patience to peel off that fear. So we were not in a rush, but we didn't give up. I told them, 'Some day, one of them out of desperation or whatever reason, she will say, 'Let me try. My life is bad anyway.' And she will try and she will succeed. Once it happens, it will have a snowballing effect.' And it did." By 1984, Yunus had reached his goal of 50 percent of the borrowers' being women. At that point he wondered, "What was so magic about 50-50? Why not more than 50 percent women?"[5]

Yunus has called his model upside-down banking. Lending to poor people, encouraging women to borrow money, and not taking any collateral were just the beginning of how his model differed from prevailing practices. Conventional banks were located in cities and towns; he took his bank to the smallest villages. In other banks, loans were paid back after a year; borrowers from Grameen made weekly repayments. Other banks lent to unassociated individuals; each borrower at Grameen became part of a group of five that was required to attend weekly meetings led by the manager from the local branch office. Other banks had no such requirements.

And Yunus's results were different from those of other banks; his rate of repayment was 98 percent while other bank's rates hovered around 60 percent. The groups of borrowers were the centerpiece of his model and provided support for faint-hearted borrowers. Being in a group helped them, as Yunus has put it, "to feel a little more courageous in their decision-making."[6]   If one member ran into difficulty making a weekly payment, the others in the group would help her out.

In the early years, weekly meetings were held under a tree or at a borrower's house. Over time, they came to be held at the village center, and their format came to include a number of set elements besides giving out loans and collecting repayments. Each meeting began with a salute, in which all the borrowers raised their right hands to their foreheads to acknowledge the branch manager. This Grameen salute, like nearly everything that Yunus did, was misunderstood and stirred up controversy over the years. Some critics believed it showed an authoritarian or militaristic streak in Yunus. Actually, the salute was conceived because Yunus was uncomfortable when women would bow their heads and lower their eyes before men. The salute—similar to the Boy Scout salute that he had grown up with—was a culturally acceptable way for men and women to acknowledge each other. Yunus wanted women to gain some dignity by learning to look directly into the eyes of others.

After the salute, the Grameen slogan was repeated. All those at the meeting shouted in unison, "Discipline, Unity, Courage, and Hard Work—we shall follow and advance in all walks of our lives." Actually, this is a Grameen version of the Boy Scout oath that Yunus had learned as a youth back in Chittagong. This was followed by a few simple exercises, like raising their arms above their heads. The borrowers disliked these exercises, and before long they were discontinued at some sites.

When I asked Nurjahan what had struck her about Yunus back in the first years of working with him, she told me this story. One day, the two of them and some others from the bank went to a village to give out loans. "I was in a borrower's house. Yunus and several other men were outside in the courtyard. I was talking to a woman named Muriam, who asked me to give her 800 takas. I was prepared to give 500 takas. I was trying to convince her but she was not convinced. All of a sudden Yunus entered the room, and all the women turned their backs to him so he couldn't see their faces. An older woman brought him a wooden stool and he sat down and started to talk to Muriam. What happened? Why did she feel the way she did? He started in his own way and making fun. After five to six minutes the women are turning around. I saw how to convince people. I learned how to convince people. He can motivate people very easily. I will never forget that moment. Now that I knew that this was possible, it gave me great hope for the future."[7]

Nurjahan continued. "Dr. Yunus is a really nice guy. When you put him anywhere, he can connect with people. It is a god-given ability." When they would go to a village together, he would play like a kid with the children who clustered around him. He often took dirty and sick babies into his arms—something Nurjahan candidly admitted that she could not bring herself to do. And, she recalled with a chuckle, Yunus often said funny things even in the midst of the most serious negotiations.

It is clear that Yunus remains Nurjahan's hero—she speaks about him with a kind of reverence. And she is protective of him. When I asked about his first marriage, she said, "He was a very caring husband. After his wife left, he tried to bring her back, but she refused. Dr. Yunus sacrificed his own life for his people. His food is very simple. His clothing is very simple, and despite the heat there is no air conditioning in his office."

Hearing this, I began to wonder how much of an independent thinker Nurjahan was. When I inquired whether she could tell Yunus when she disagreed with him, she smiled at me and said sharply, "Of course." [8]

She herself, she explained, had been very fortunate in life, able to break free of many of the constraints that limited women in the countryside and even middle-class women like her mother. She had a university education, had married a man of her own choosing, had planned the size of her family—one child, and had worked her entire life. Truly a pioneer, I decided.

In those first years of the Grameen Bank Project, while women staff members like Nurjahan were trying to adapt to the world of work, Yunus was struggling to convince the banking world of the merits of his model. In 1978, he gave a talk about his project at a conference in Bangladesh sponsored by the U.S. Agency for International Development (USAID). In two pages he outlined his successes and presented data to back up the claim that he had a 98 percent repayment rate. He asked the audience, "What does our experience mean?"[9] The bureaucrats and academics were sure that his success depended on his personal charisma and the fact that he was well known in the Jobra area. One banker at the meeting insisted that, to really prove anything about his model, Yunus needed to try it out in an area far away and make it work in an entire district where he was unknown. Yunus accepted the challenge on the spot, on condition that he would get the funding and resources necessary for such a major expansion.

Although the deputy governor of the Bangladesh Bank, Asit Kumar Gangopadhaya, who was present at the meeting, was impressed by Yunus, the key people from the other nationalized banks remained skeptical. To get them on board with the idea of supporting his expansion, Yunus took a group of them to Jobra. Seeing his project for themselves and hearing the stories from a number of borrowers turned the tide. The directors of the Bangladesh Bank, along with six other banks, agreed to provide the funding and resources that Yunus would need to expand into an entire district. Such financial support was necessary because, although once the

Project was up and running it would be self-sustaining, the start-up phase would be costly.

For the expansion, the directors chose the district of Tangail, 70 miles north of Dhaka and far from Chittagong, where Yunus was known. Each of the seven nationalized banks agreed to provide space for the Grameen Bank Project at several of their branches, creating a total of 19 sites. The bankers insisted that, to be granted the space and some funding, Yunus had to quit his university job and become a full-time banker. He agreed to take a two-year leave of absence from the Chittagong University and to move to Tangail. He figured that if his model were a success, the banks would, of course, begin lending to the poor throughout Bangladesh. If it failed, he could always return to teaching at the university.

Tangail was a troubled district. Violent left-wing Marxist groups called the People's Army roamed the countryside terrorizing the populace. It was not unusual to see dead bodies, victims of these groups, left lying in the middle of the road. Yunus was not deterred.

He had initially agreed to use staff already employed at the existing banks to work at his project. Of course, since most of them didn't understand his mission, they were uncooperative or even hostile. So he installed several of his former students to oversee the Project and to hire the additional new staff that would be required. Each new site was staffed by a manager, a guard, and five bank workers. The Project's central office was modest—a few tables and chairs, some file cabinets, and one typewriter. Yunus lived in a tiny rented room near the office and ate his meals in the communal mess they set up—a stark contrast from the comforts of his home in Chittagong.

He put Nurjahan in charge of the women staff. Her mother was upset at the idea of her leaving home and moving to Tangail; it was just not acceptable for a single woman to live on her own. But since her mother did not know where Tangail was, she agreed to let her go when Nurjahan told her she would be spending nights with her brother, who lived in Dhaka. In reality, this was not possible, as Tangail was many hours away from Dhaka by bus.

When Nurjahan arrived in Tangail, she found that no one would rent a room to an unmarried woman. Finally, she found a woman who worked at CARE who would let her stay at her house. It was rather far from the office, which meant Nurjahan had to walk home from evening meetings in the dark, alone.

Living in Tangail was difficult for Yunus, too. He worked all the time and had no time for personal life. Some of his friends worried about him and thought he should marry again, and in 1980 they began looking for a suitable bride. They settled on a woman named Afrosi Begum and arranged the marriage for them. Afrosi was a researcher in advanced physics at the University of Manchester in England and was used to living in a developed country as well as in Bangladesh. After the wedding, which was a traditional Bangladeshi event, Afrosi returned to Manchester to finish out a term before joining Yunus in his simple quarters in Tangail.

When I first heard that Yunus's second marriage had been arranged, I was puzzled and, to be frank, disappointed. It seemed inconceivable to me that he, whose loans helped liberate millions of women, would let others select a mate for him and choose to stay with the outmoded practice of an arranged marriage. Of course, this is an American perspective; I am aware that many millions of people in the world continue to have arranged marriages. And after some pondering, and learning more about Yunus, I realized that it made sense. In Tangail, he was working day after day from dawn to dusk, focused on proving to the world that his model could work anywhere. At this point, his personal life was not a priority, and a long courtship that took him away from Tangail must have seemed out of the question.

Perhaps most important, I came to see that Yunus was not trying to destroy the Bangladeshi traditional way of life. He never talks about liberation as the goal, only alleviating poverty. His upside-down banking, which broke with so many conventional practices, was a means to this end. And, of course, his first marriage, which had been untraditional and not supported by his family, had ended badly.

People describe Afrosi as shy, quiet, preferring to stay home. Their daughter Deena was born in 1986. In 2010 she was living with Yunus and Afrosi in Dhaka and, according to my sources, was uncertain about her career direction. She is still finding herself according to Yunus. Though Afrosi is now retired from research and teaching, she rarely travels with Yunus. When I asked him about interviewing her, he looked pained and asked me not to bother her, though he gave me his daughter Monica's telephone number with no hesitation.

The political climate in Tangail was one of unrest. At times Yunus was worried about the safety of his staff. Several times he was shocked to discover his own staff walking around with machine guns hidden in their garments. It turned out they were former members of the People's Army! Many of the original staff at the existing banks continued to create problems for the Grameen staff. Yunus spent long days touring the district in a jeep, sitting in on center meetings and talking with borrowers. He was determined to grow his project.

The expansion went even better than he had hoped. In 1979 there had been a total of 500 borrowers; by the end of 1981 there were 22,000—a quantum jump in less than two years. By the end of 1982 there were 30,000 borrowers. The model was working in Tangail just as it had in Chittagong.

Word about the effectiveness of the Grameen Bank Project was spreading. In 1980 the International Agency for Agricultural Development (IFAD) offered to lend Yunus $3.4 million on condition that the Bangladesh Bank would match their loan. The money could be used to expand into an additional two districts beyond Tangail. A member of the Bangladesh Bank's board, A.M.A. Muhith, was designated to give the final authorization. Muhith and Yunus knew each other well; they had worked together for the Bangladeshi cause in Washington, D.C., in the summer of 1971. Despite their prior relationship, Muhith was not convinced that the Grameen model was practical. So Yunus persuaded him to come to Tangail to see for himself how the Grameen Bank Project looked in the field. Once again, seeing the Project worked magic.

Muhith remembered his visit this way. "In the villages, I saw Yunus in a totally new light. ... The people's response to him was overwhelming. He would say something—anything—and it immediately registered." Muhith had wondered whether there was a market for all the goods and services that the loans from Grameen had spawned. And then he understood: "They had become each other's customers."[10] After the loan was approved, Yunus moved his office to Dhaka as he expanded into the new districts.

By 1982 it had dawned on Yunus that what he really wanted was for his Project to become an independent bank. The current arrangements where he shared space in existing banks in Tangail weren't working. He continued to lose staff, in part because of the lack of respect shown them by the employees of the government banks.

All the directors of the national banks in Bangladesh opposed the idea of an independent Grameen Bank, and they were joined by many others—bankers at every rank, politicians on the far right and on the far left. Their reasons for opposition were many and often contradictory. Grameen was delaying a Marxist revolution by giving false hope to the poor; credit was not really bringing about much change; the model was not sustainable since it depended on Yunus; the markets could not support so many small businesses; and no scientific study had proved Yunus's model was effective.

In March of 1982, everything changed suddenly when General Hossain Mohammed Ershad staged a coup d'etat and placed Bangladesh under military rule. This distressing development had an upside for Yunus. General Ershad selected Muhith, the very man who had recently helped Yunus get the $3.4 million loan, to be his finance minister. Yunus knew when to take action and when to be patient, and now was a time to move fast. He went to Muhith and explained why it was important for

Grameen to become an independent bank and why the government should own 40 percent of the bank and the borrowers 60 percent. Yunus was never troubled that the borrowers were uneducated and illiterate. Muhith liked the idea of the government doing something for the poor and promised to do what he could.

Muhith recalled years later, "I had the support of only one person in government—Ershad. But at the time, the government was Ershad."[11] Muhith got Ershad to approve the plan for the Grameen Bank's independence; but at the last minute, he switched the percentages so that the government owned 60 percent of the Grameen Bank and the borrowers only 40 percent. Yunus was outraged, but calmed down when Muhith explained that the deal wouldn't have gone through otherwise. He assured Yunus that the ownership percentages could change over time.

Since the decision still had to go through the formalities of acceptance by Parliament, Yunus was afraid the foot dragging could last for years. But in September of 1983, the Grameen Bank Ordinance was passed and Grameen became an independent bank. Yunus could now manage as he wished, free from the interference of other bankers and free to expand as fast and as far as he could.

You might conclude that Yunus was born under a lucky star. At so many points as he was trying to establish his bank, an ally like Howlader, Anisuzzaman, Gangopadhaya, or Muhith would appear on the scene at just the right moment to save the day.

As a social psychologist, I see it differently. Yunus knew how to create allies. In spite of considering himself shy, he had an uncanny ability to create a relationship quickly. Often people he had just met would become committed to his cause and willing to go to unbelievable lengths to help him. Was it charisma, his warmth, his good-nature, his humor, or his mission to alleviate poverty? In my view, it was all of them and more. Yunus knew how to create his lucky breaks. He had a sixth sense that guided him as he faced one challenge after another—he might make a big fuss, accept a temporary setback, or take action.

Achieving legal status for Grameen as an independent bank gave a huge boost to Yunus's operations and his dream of expansion. He had more freedom to manage, as he had wanted, and his independent status made it more difficult for the government to intervene.

And Nurjahan was there to help Yunus with further expansion of the Bank. At one point in the years before Grameen gained its independence, officials from the government had offered her a position. She seriously considered accepting it, since the Project might fail and in a few years her options would diminish as she would be over the age limit for entering government service.

When she told Yunus about her job offer, he said, "Don't apply for any more jobs, we need you here." And that is all it took for Nurjahan to stay. For 30 years, she and Yunus and would face an endless series of challenges— and see the spread of the Grameen model beyond their wildest dreams. For many of those years, as the highest ranking woman at the Grameen Bank, she oversaw administration and the training of all new hires. In 2009, with the sudden departure of Dipal Barua, Yunus's second in command, Nurjahan was named deputy managing director of the fabled Grameen Bank. What a remarkable journey she has taken from that day in 1977 when she had told Yunus she wanted to quit.

Women borrowers attend the required weekly meeting.

Bishaka Rani Das and her flourishing chicken business.

Chapter Seven:

Touching Money for the First Time

"**Y**ou will definitely want to go to a weekly meeting in a village," declared Lamiya Morshed as we planned my schedule for that week in January, 2010.[1] Lamiya runs the Yunus Centre, which is the Grameen Bank's face to the outside world. Yes, of course I wanted to get out to the field, and no, $50 was not too much to pay for a car, a driver, and a person from the bank to accompany me. I was eager to see for myself what life was like for village women in Bangladesh, and I was especially interested in observing the impact that getting a loan from the Grameen Bank had on their lives.

But a few days later, as I was being driven out of Dhaka in a Grameen car in the pitch black early morning, I found myself getting tense. Would I be seen as an American voyeur come to gawk at unfortunate poor people? Would I be able to connect to the village women? Would I catch some horrible skin disease or a deadly virus in the village? Did I have enough bottled water to last the day? And then I thought, Katharine, you are really a wimp to be so anxious about a one-day trip. Just think about people like Alex Counts and Helen Todd, whom I had read about, who had spent months and years living in remote villages in Bangladesh, hours from a city or a hospital.

* * * * *

It had been Yunus's belief in the potential of poor people, and especially poor women, that had drawn me to him in the first place. Yunus has often compared people who are poor to bonsai trees. "There is nothing wrong with their seeds, but society never gave them the proper base to grow on. All it takes to get poor people out of poverty is for us to create an enabling environment for them. Once the poor can unleash their energy and creativity, poverty will disappear very quickly."[2] He talks frequently, as well, about the unrecognized skills of the poor. "The fact that they are alive is clear proof of their ability. They do not need us to teach them how to survive. ... Giving the poor access to credit allows them to immediately put into practice the skills they already know—to weave, husk rice, raise cows, pedal a rickshaw. And the cash they earn is a tool, a key that unlocks a host of other abilities and allows them to explore their own potential."[3]

While others saw the poor, and especially the landless poor in Bangladesh, as stupid or lazy, in need of training, handouts, and help from the government, Yunus has always maintained that what the poor need most is capital, capital to start or grow a business. He believes everyone has the potential to be an entrepreneur and succeed in running a small business. He has insisted it is really much simpler than most development experts believe. I have always wondered about that. Is Yunus right about the power of credit? Have others just been complicating things unnecessarily?

After about an hour of driving in silence, the driver pulled over to the side of the road beside a man sitting on shiny new motorcycle and sporting a rainbow-colored helmet. My Grameen guide for the day introduced me to Mijanur Rahman, a branch manager who would escort us to the center meeting. Rahman gunned his bike, and we bumped slowly along behind him down a narrow dirt lane. After about 20 minutes, we stopped in a grassy field. Rahman led us, now on foot, down a hard-packed dirt path past a pond on one side, toward a cluster of trees and a wooden shed with a tin roof—the Grameen center.

As we drew close, I heard peals of laughter and the pleasant sound of women's voices. When I was ushered into the meeting, what I noticed was a blur of the mostly red, green, and blue saris, jackets, and scarves. About 30 women were huddled on the center's wooden benches. Many of them were bouncing babies on their laps as they chatted. They smiled at me as we entered. This was not exactly the picture of poverty I had anticipated. I felt the tension flow out of my body.

* * * * *

Yunus had discovered during the first decade of Grameen's independence that the Bank could keep on attracting new borrowers. Pilot projects usually flounder when there are attempts to replicate an amazing success. Not so with Yunus and the Grameen Bank. Each year, Yunus was able to launch nearly a hundred new branches. In 1983 there had been 86 branches and 58,000 borrowers; by 1995 there were 1,055 branches and more than two million borrowers. And Yunus continued to report repayment rates that were above 97 percent.

It was not, however, a decade without setbacks. In 1984, Yunus got word of trouble at one of the branches in Tangail. He immediately dispatched a team to investigate. To his great dismay, the team discovered that some of his staff had been stealing from borrowers, skimming money off their deposits, and lying to them about their status. He knew that the Grameen Bank depended on trust, and now he feared that its reputation for integrity was tarnished. With special efforts over several years, the troubled branch was gradually brought back into the fold, but Yunus realized he had to be even more vigilant in guarding against the corruption that was typical of Bangladeshi institutions.

Although he believed that borrowers did not need lengthy skills training or education before they received their first loans, Yunus did insist that each new borrower go through a period of studying the Bank's rules and regulations. This was followed by an oral examination to be sure new borrowers understood their understood their responsibility to start a new business or grow an existing one. A small part of each first loan was used by the borrower to acquire one share of the bank. So getting a loan from Grameen also entailed becoming an owner of the bank, a role far beyond what most village women could even imagine or comprehend. And Yunus was thrilled that over the years, he was able to negotiate to increase the percentage of the Bank's shares that borrowers owed to 75 percent while shrinking the government's ownership to 25 percent.

Every year Yunus brought a large group of borrowers together for workshops to discuss common issues and to support each other. At these annual workshops, participants developed a few decisions that all borrowers would agree to live by. By 1984 borrowers had come up with sixteen decisions, and Yunus urged them to stop before the number became unwieldy. Since then, the Sixteen Decisions have been read or recited from time to time at some branches of the Grameen Bank. At the center meeting I attended, borrowers sat clutching worn copies of the Sixteen Decisions as if they were their most prized possessions or a holy text.

The Sixteen Decisions

1.   The four principles of Grameen Bank—Discipline, Unity, Courage, and Hard Work—we shall follow and advance in all walks of our lives.

2. Prosperity we shall bring to our families.

3. We shall not live in dilapidated houses. We shall repair our houses and work toward constructing new houses at the earliest.

4. We shall grow vegetables all the year round. We shall eat plenty of them and sell the surplus.

5. During the plantation seasons, we shall plant as many seedlings as possible.

6. We shall plan to keep our families small. We shall minimize our expenditures. We shall look after our health.

7. We shall educate our children and ensure that they can earn to pay for their education.

8. We shall always keep our children and the environment clean.

9. We shall build and use pit-latrines.

10. We shall drink tubewell water. If it is not available, we shall boil water or use alum to purify it.

11. We shall not take any dowry in our sons' weddings, neither shall we give any dowry in our daughters' weddings. We shall keep the center free from the curse of dowry. We shall not practice child marriage.

12. We shall not inflict any injustice on anyone, neither shall we allow anyone to do so.

13. For higher income we shall collectively undertake bigger investments.

14. We shall always be ready to help each other. If anyone is in difficulty, we shall all help him. *her?*

15. If we come to know of any breach of discipline in any center, we shall all go there and help restore discipline.

16. We shall introduce physical exercise in all our centers. We shall take part in all social activities collectively.[4]

Americans may not generally realize the degree to which the Sixteen Decisions challenged the status quo in rural Bangladesh. It is not an exaggeration to claim that the behavioral changes that borrowers agreed to ignited a social revolution. Asking borrowers to eliminate the dowry, for example, was asking them to break with a fundamental tradition that was woven into the social fabric. Most families started putting away savings for the wedding of a daughter on the day she was born; it was a point of honor to send the bride off with as large a dowry as they could possibly afford.

The dowry, however, had led to serious problems for generations. Some men sent their wives home to their parents so they could marry for a second time and get another dowry. Or if the dowry money was slow in coming, the wife might die in a kitchen "accident." Many hundreds of women still die each year from these kinds of deaths. Similarly, the idea of family planning to keep a family small ran counter to the conventional wisdom of a thousand years that more children meant more security. Sending their kids to school, building latrines, and fixing up their houses were nice aspirations, but usually far beyond the reach of poor women. Yunus understood this, and there were no institutional consequences for failures to abide by the Sixteen Decisions.

When I asked Yunus about the impact of the Sixteen Decisions, he responded, "Who are we to say? You can ask how important is it to go to church. You go there. You come back and do the same old thing. You don't change a bit. But hopefully the sermon that the priest gives holds one or two hours of your attention and then something will happen. So the Sixteen Decisions did not change everything, but some people took it seriously, half seriously. If it works, I didn't spend anything for that."[5]

Both by lending to women and by requiring them to attempt to live by the Sixteen Decisions, Yunus was encouraging changes in lifestyle patterns that had lasted for centuries. While a shift in gender dynamics per se may not have been his intention, it was certainly a result. It was during these years that the Grameen Bank made the transition from being a bank for the poor to becoming a bank for poor women, as the percentage of borrowers who were women grew steadily until it was 94 percent in 1995.

Yunus created other policies at the Grameen Bank that gave explicit power to women rather than men. For example, the Bank began to give loans for housing as well as for small businesses, and it was a stipulation of the loan that the house had to be entirely owned by the woman rather than by the man, which was the norm. Despite the shock and resistance that this policy created, Yunus held firm. Women who became owners gained enormous clout, and the likelihood that their husbands would abandon them decreased significantly.

Yunus has rarely discussed the impact of being a member of a small group of women borrowers or how they were changed by attending the required weekly meetings. Nor does he often talk about women's empowerment as a goal. It is my view that for many women borrowers of Grameen the impact of the group experience and the socialization at the weekly meetings has been just as important as receiving a small loan.

There is a large body of psychological research that confirms the power of groups to shift attitudes and opinions. Equally persuasive to me is my experience as a social psychologist leading hundreds of groups—therapy groups, training programs, and group strategic planning sessions. Over and over, I have witnessed how people change their attitudes and behaviors in the context of a group where they feel safe. In a supportive group, people become more open and more trusting.

Twenty-Seven Dollars and a Dream

Imagine a woman in rural Bangladesh, who typically never left her family compound. She never went to markets or the next town or to visit neighbors—until she married, when she moved to her husband's village and lived with his family. Her social interactions thereafter were by custom limited to her husband's female relatives. People rarely spoke to others of a different social status or clan, and most people were suspicious of everyone outside the extended family circle.

Becoming a Grameen borrower meant that each week a woman needed to walk to the center meeting, sometimes miles away. There she spent a couple of hours with a group of women who were unrelated to her. There the bank staff called each borrower by her first name. This was very different from the way women were usually addressed in their homes, which was in terms of their male relatives—as So-and-So's wife or So-and-So's daughter. Just hearing their names forged a new sense of identity for these women. Some girls in rural Bangladesh were never given a name, a tradition that explains, by the way, why having a name was one of the rights established by the UN Declaration of the Rights of the Child in 1959.

A lot happened at a Grameen center weekly meeting, which typically consisted of six to eight small groups of five women each. While the leaders of the small groups handed in repayment money, the other women chatted with those in their small groups as well as the 30 or so other women at the meeting. They compared notes on how their businesses were doing, gave each other tips, and passed along news and gossip. A new world opened up for most of them.

Lisa Larance, an American who spent a year in Bangladesh in the 1990s, studied the social impact of the Grameen Bank meetings at two centers. Among other findings, she learned that 75 percent of the 80 women she studied made new friends and, after getting a loan and beginning to attend weekly center meetings, began to visit these friends on a daily or weekly basis. They described lending clothing or jewelry to these new friends and giving them advice. They had broken out of the isolation of the traditional life of village women and were part of a new social network.

* * * * *

Alex Counts was one of the early visitors to Grameen from the United States who came to study the impact of the small loans, or microcredit as this process was now called. An economics major at Cornell, Counts had a professor who taught him that every problem has been solved somewhere and you need to look for those small successes. When Counts read about Yunus, he was impressed. He wrote asking whether he could come and work at the Grameen Bank for a year. Yunus's reply was blunt. Counts could come, but would have to pay his way and would get no salary. "If you don't like the work, you can leave,"Yunus wrote. "If we don't like you, we will not be able to use you."[6]

When Counts actually arrived in Bangladesh in 1989, on a Fulbright, it was a different story right from the start. Yunus took great interest in him, carefully read Counts's lengthy reports of his observations of how microcredit was working in the field, and gave him feedback. Then he started asking for Counts's opinions. He realized that the young man had given a lot of thought to Grameen's operations and potential and was serious about dedicating his life to Yunus's mission. Counts had even learned to speak fluent Bangla, as the language in Bangladesh was now called, something few Americans have ever done.

Counts came to Bangladesh a second time to conduct more research for a book that would get the Grameen story out to a wider public. He spent days and months in small villages observing the Grameen Bank in action and getting personally acquainted with many of the borrowers and their situations. Counts's book, *Give Us Credit: How Muhammad Yunus's Micro-Lending Revolution Is Empowering Women from Bangladesh to Chicago*, was published in 1996. Incidentally, the Chicago replication of the Grameen model, which Counts chronicled in great detail, floundered for several years and then withered away.

In 1997, Yunus gave Counts a few thousand dollars to start the Grameen Foundation in Washington, D.C., to fund replications of Grameen around the world. Since then, the Foundation has flourished under Counts's leadership. More about replications in a later chapter.

One of the people who Counts follows in his book *Give Us Credit*, later reissued as *Small Loans, Big Dreams*, is a woman named Amena Begum. Her experience suggests how individual lives have been affected by a loan from the Grameen Bank.[7]

In 1993, a Hindu neighbor told Amena Begum, a young Muslim woman, that there were openings in the Grameen Bank Group #7 in their village of Kholshoi. Group #7 had recently failed its entrance examination and three members had dropped out. Amena's neighbor encouraged her to join the group and take out a loan. Although Amena was pregnant with her fifth child, she decided to do it. Her life was difficult anyway. Her husband, Absar Ali, beat her almost daily and often threatened to take a second wife. Amena had a nasty scar on her face from the time he had hit her with a bicycle chain. Absar Ali sold aluminum pots and pans, but his business was not doing well. The couple had moved to Kholshoi in western Bangladesh after their home had been washed away by the powerful Ganges River. They squatted on a small piece of land owned by Amena's grandfather and were able to build a small home—a hut, really—for about $200. There was no money for furniture, so the house was empty.

Having decided to take out a small loan, Amena studied diligently for the group entrance exam. Since she had gone to school through third grade, she learned more easily than those in the group who had had no schooling at all. On the day of their exam, they all were nervous because of their earlier failure. The manager who came to test them was tired when he arrived, late in the day. He turned to one of the women and asked, "What is Decision #9?" Luckily, she was able to respond quickly, "We shall build and use pit-latrines." Then, tossing aside the usual protocol, he announced to the astonished group that they had passed the test. The final step was the inspection of all the homes of the new group members, to be sure they were essentially landless and poor enough to qualify. The Grameen Bank was firm about serving only the poorest of the poor. Clearly Amena's hut did not disqualify them.

The night before Amena was to get her first loan, she went into labor and delivered a baby boy on the floor of her hut. Two weeks later she was able to walk the three miles to the center meeting to collect her first loan of 3,000 takas. She gave Absar Ali 1,900 takas to buy pots and pans, although she knew that was against the rules; her loan was supposed to support only her own small business. One hundred takas went to buy her share of the Grameen Bank and for an emergency fund. The rest she squirreled away to buy ducks, ducklings, and chickens. She built her business in secret so that her husband wouldn't get wind of how much money she was making.

Absar Ali was happy because for the first time he had the cash to buy pots and pans without going to a moneylender. Amena sent her young daughter to the nearby markets to sell eggs, thrilled to be able to pocket a little extra cash each week and have a few eggs for the children to eat.

Then Amena's Hindu neighbor came up with another idea: Amena should tell Absar Ali that the Grameen Bank did not give second loans to families where the wife was regularly beaten. The ruse worked like a charm. Over the next few months, Absar Ali stopped beating Amena.

Emboldened by her success, Amena took out another loan, this time for a tubewell so she could irrigate her vegetable garden. She had to pump 20 buckets each day and carry the water over to the garden, but it was worth it, as the pumpkins, beans, chilis, eggplant, and spinach flourished. Soon after this, she succeeded in getting yet another loan, to buy a cow. Now she had some milk for the children, and the profits from her secret business were growing along with the garden.

Then Amena's brother, who pulled rickshaws in Dhaka, was killed. The neighbors said it was Allah's

revenge because he had eloped with a married woman.
These neighbors made life so unpleasant for the family
that Amena's parents and Absar Ali wanted to move away.
Amena was devastated, because it had looked as though
her life had finally turned around. After many discussions,
she was finally able to persuade them to stay. And in
fact, the family continued to prosper. The next year
Amena sold a cow and made a big profit. In 2005, the
family did move away from Kholshi to a suburb of Dhaka.
Amena reluctantly had to give up her connection to the
Grameen Bank, as the Bank was not legally permitted to
operate in urban settings.

Amena was one of the Grameen stars—someone who
made progress right from the start. There were many
others who did not fare so well. Their cows stopped
lactating, or there was sickness in the family and all
their savings were wiped out. In Amena's Group #7,
for example, one woman had to drop out because she
couldn't keep up with her payments, and two others had
more setbacks than successes.

However, while there were some women whose
loans did not work out well, there were more—many
thousands of women like Amena, all across Bangladesh—
who flourished with the additional opportunities their
loans provided.

Ever since word of Yunus's astonishing successes
seeped out to the wider world, there have been bankers,

journalists, development experts, and academics who have wanted to learn about the impact of microcredit on the lives of women. Yunus told me in an interview, "There are lots of studies done on Grameen Bank. Tons and tons of studies. Because people are curious. They say, 'He is fooling everybody. And I'm going to find out the truth.' So they came in with a big research team and in the process they start understanding and seeing it. By the time their research is done, they become great admirers of Grameen. So our shelves are filling up with reports, books, theses, articles, dissertations."[8]

Yunus went on to explain, "Then there was another class of researchers who came saying extremely negative things. Everybody wants to find some fault with Grameen, and they found it. They reported that 'It's true: the Grameen Bank tightens the screws to get the money back. They bond their houses. They're so tough with their women. The women don't use the money, it's the husbands that use it… They are tools in the hands of men.'"[9]

Helen Todd, a journalist, and her husband, David Gibbons, a professor of political science who had worked on a Grameen replication in Malaysia, were among those interested in learning about the long-term impact of Grameen loans. Focusing on two villages, they recruited a group of 40 women who had borrowed at least ten times from the Grameen Bank. Then they created a control group of 24 women who would have qualified to get a loan from the Bank ten years earlier but had chosen not to. All 64 households were poor. During most of 1992, Todd lived in one of the villages and Gibbons in the other. With the help of a researcher, they conducted weekly interviews with each of the 64 subjects.

Todd and Gibbons found it was true that many of the borrowers were using their loans for purposes different from what they had proposed to the Bank. Many of them did give their money to their husbands, as Amena had done, or bought land—which was not permitted. Yunus believed that if borrowers were allowed to buy land it would increase poverty because they would be buying from the poorest landowners, who would be forced to sell their only asset in a time of crisis such as an illness in the family.

On the positive side, Todd and Gibbons found that on average, women who were Grameen borrowers contributed 54 percent of the total family earnings compared to 25 percent by non-borrowers. The children of borrowers were a bit taller and heavier, though all the children were still underweight by World Health Organization standards. Fifty-eight percent of the Grameen borrowers had moved out of the official category of extreme poverty by being able to provide 1,800 calories to each family member per day; only 25 percent of those in the control group had been able to do so. The researchers also discovered that 60 percent

of those borrowers who were still in the extreme
poverty category had confronted a serious illness like
tuberculosis or typhoid in the family.

Todd found that the borrowers in their study were,
for the most part, implementing those of the Sixteen
Decisions that concerned health. For example, all the
borrowers in both groups were drinking safe water
from the tubewells. Twenty-one percent of the Grameen
women used sanitary latrines, while none of the control
group did. Ninety-six percent of the Grameen women
were growing vine vegetables compared with 63 percent
of the control group. The Grameen women immunized
more of their children, 85 percent, compared to the
control group, which immunized 66 percent.

Todd writes, "The main meaning of the center to the
women in our sample is as a window for credit to pursue
their individual self-interest, firmly rooted in their primary
loyalties to their families." But she was also impressed by
those other changes in the Grameen borrowers, including
some that were not captured by statistics. She observed
shifts in the family dynamics, with women gaining
influence over time. She writes, "GB (Grameen Bank)
women effect change more like termites, hollowing out
structures quietly from within rather than pushing them
over…. There is no doubt that ten years of attending
meetings, articulating loan proposals, dealing with male
bank workers, and walking to town to visit the branch
office has given the women an awareness and self-

confidence in addition to the self-esteem they get from the economic contribution."[10]

In David Bornstein's *The Price of a Dream:The Story of the Grameen Bank*, which was published in 1996, he quotes a Grameen manager:"At the branch the difference between a new borrower and a four or five-year borrower is very evident. At the beginning, they don't know where to sit, what to do, who to talk to. Later they just come in, they know everybody, they go about their business, signing or asking for the money or arguing back sometimes. In the center meetings, new borrowers hardly look up and they don't speak up. Older ones are chatting away. If the bank worker doesn't agree, they'll argue, they'll go to the manager. They know what needs to be done.... The husband agrees more often or at least doesn't contradict her."[11]

Todd's study is still cited because of her in-depth understanding and her inclusion of a control group. These gave it traction. Her findings could not be so easily tossed aside by the critics of Yunus as some of the earlier evaluations of Grameen.

Yunus steered clear of arguments about the impact of the Grameen Bank and the degree to which women were empowered by their small loans. He just concentrated on expanding his number of borrowers. Originally I had seen him through the lens of my own perspective. Aha, I thought when I first met him. This is fantastic. A Muslim man who is also feminist. And in Bangladesh, no less. As I came to understand him better, I had to give up my wish that he was a feminist by ideology, concerned first and foremost about equality for women. It is obvious that the policies of the Bank supported women's development; it just wasn't his primary goal. That doesn't mean he hasn't been instrumental in empowering millions of woman. He has.

Todd says the stereotypes about the women that she had when she began her study—that they were passive and uninterested in improving their lives—were shattered. The women she came know were resourceful, funny, and different from each other.

Her comments resonated with my experience at that center meeting, where what I first noticed was women laughing and smiling. After the meeting, Bishaka Rani Das, the assistant leader and apparently the oldest member, rushed up to me and escorted me outside to meet her son, who was in his fourth year of college (the equivalent of our high school) on a Grameen Bank scholarship. She took a picture of him and me and then, grinning broadly and showing her mostly toothless smile, insisted, "Now you must see my chickens—a thousand chickens!" To this day when I think of women's empowerment and Grameen, it is the image of Bishaka Rani Das grinning at me in front of her chicken coop that comes to mind.

Yunus in the 1980s cutting the ribbon as another center is launched.

A branch manager in his small office in 2010.

Chapter Eight:

Practical Visionary

$\mathbf{Y}$unus is one of those rare individuals who has excelled as both a leader and a manager. He was able to create a vision that inspired generations of employees and borrowers for over thirty years. He used his charisma and the loyalty of his employees, but never relied solely on them. He also developed management systems to ensure that the organization worked smoothly and that people were held accountable. In contrast to Yunus, most CEOs are unable to keep their organizations flourishing for even a single decade.

"When I went back to work for Yunus, I didn't even ask what my job would be or what salary I would get," H.I. Latifee recalled as we sat shivering in his unheated office at the Grameen Bank during my visit to Bangladesh in 2010.[1] Yes, he had actually agreed to go back to work for Yunus in 1993, after a decade away, without knowing what he would be doing.

Latifee had told Yunus that he would be able to start in June. Yunus had responded, "Why not sooner, why not January?" Latifee arrived for his new job on January 1st because Yunus had asked him to. And it was only then that he learned that Yunus wanted him to be the managing director of the Grameen Trust, which offers training and technical assistance to support Grameen Bank replications in Bangladesh and internationally. Toward the end of the first month, Latifee's staff asked what they should record as his salary in their budget reports. When he said he didn't know, they were incredulous and asked him to get the information from Yunus immediately. Latifee replied, "No, this is not my headache. Do you think I came for the money? I have come here for a cause and because Professor Yunus wants me here. He is not a person to forget things, he is very responsible."[2] And on January 28 Yunus sent out a memo with full details of Latifee's salary and benefits.

Latifee recalled the early days of the Bank and how Yunus spoke to young staff members who were worried about committing to the Grameen Bank since its future was so uncertain. He would always tell them it was their life and they should feel free to make the decision that was right for them. But he would always add that the work they were doing at the Bank was the most important work in Bangladesh. "This is the work that the country needs."[3]

A few days later in January 2010, when I asked Yunus about his view of leadership, he had plenty to say. "A leader is someone who sees ahead, is captain of the ship. He has to know whether he'll find the land. The crew is frustrated... All they see is water. The captain says, 'No, there's land out there. Let's move on. ... 'You don't know anything, but you give the feeling to your crew it exists, and they work for it. ... Leadership is about seeing in the distance. It's about vision and transmitting that vision to your followers."[4]

Yunus admitted that he knew achieving his goals was not going to happen easily or right away. "I had lots of contingency plans. If Plan A doesn't work, Plan B doesn't work, Plan C, and so on, so I am making all those preparations."[5]

Latifee was obviously a great admirer of Yunus's management skills as well as his leadership. He said, "Yunus has the power to get things done. He trusts people and believes every human being has unlimited potential. If you give a person responsibility, they will perform."

Asif Dowla is another person who emphasized to me what a skilled manager Yunus has been. Dowla, a Bangladeshi who left the Bank, is now professor at St. Mary's College of Maryland. He described Yunus as a hands-on manager who spent his days working his way through an enormous to-do list. "He always responds to every email."[6]

Like so many in Yunus's circle, Dowla first met him in the '70s when Yunus was his professor at Chittagong University. Dowla was impressed by his teaching; Yunus was able to give statistics a philosophical twist. He also thought Yunus dashing, with his nicely tailored jackets, colorful ties, and long hair. After graduating from the university, Dowla had to wait two or three months before he could start his new job as a professor. Yunus met him in the corridor one day and hired him to start working at the Bank the next day. Yunus was not one to get bogged down by red tape, and he trusted his intuition.

Later on, when Dowla was teaching in Chittagong, he would often run into Yunus, who was visiting from Tangail. At first Dowla was in awe of his former teacher, but gradually they became colleagues. Dowla remembers how often they would buy some peanuts and go for a long walk. "Yunus would quiz me about things. He wanted to know what was happening in academic circles since he didn't have time to understand the debate in depth. Government regulation in Bangladesh was a big topic of the day and one about which he had strong views. I remember him saying, 'You don't need a traffic light when you are still driving a cart.'"[7]

Dowla remembers that Yunus refused many invitations to participate in conferences and give speeches because he was busy attending to matters at the Bank. He kept in close touch with his managers, carefully studying the reports they all sent him each week. This was not a check-list kind of report; Yunus insisted managers write a lengthy narrative describing what was happening at their sites. This is how he learned what needed his attention. In the early years, he also toured the countryside, holding meetings with staff and borrowers to listen to their issues and concerns. He had made a decision to visit every single branch of the Bank at least once and was able to do that until there were more than 600 of them.

When I asked Yunus about his thoughts on management, he responded, "I would say that my management style is to let the staff feel that they are telling me rather than I'm telling them. So even if I have some idea, I don't come up and tell the idea. I said, 'How can this thing happen? What do you think? Yeah. You're right. You added a little bit. But that's a great idea. I like that. What do you think?' So, gradually, I try to bring them to that image that I already have in mind, so everybody's putting a piece into it. I say, 'That's what we should do. You're wonderful.' So I'm trying to push them to the direction that I had already planned out. ... So in the end they say, 'I did it.'"[8]

I felt a bit disturbed by the last riff—it sounded more like the pretense of participative management than participative management. Back in the States, I had to fight the impulse to cut this quote because Yunus's idea of participative management differed significantly from mine and I thought his comment made him sound manipulative. But I caught myself and gave myself a short lecture on objective reporting.

Yunus went on to explain that he was adamant that practices and procedures be followed exactly the same way in every branch, every center, no matter where they were located. "Everybody's on the front line and everybody knows exactly what to do," he insisted.[9] But by 1998, there were more than two million members and over 1100 branches, so this was an enormous task. Part of what made it possible was the modular structure of the Bank. As noted earlier, the basic building block was the small group of five borrowers, with each center serving six to eight small groups. A branch consisted of 60 centers, and 10 branches reported to an area office. Ten areas reported to zone managers, who in turn reported to the Head Office.

Yunus explained to me how this organization worked. "Each branch is independent in financial terms and in decision making. They have certain criteria to judge their performance. Is their repayment rate high, close enough to 100 percent? Are the borrowers having an easy time, fun time paying it back, or do they have to really put pressure on them in some way?" He would ask a manager, "'Are you mad at any borrower? If you're mad at any borrower, something is wrong in your system. It's your fault. It's not her fault. ... Don't get mad at the people. Get mad at the way you did it. And correct it so that it works well. So always take the blame yourself.'"[10]

Most bankers don't talk to their staff like this. Some people might dismiss Yunus's comments as demonstrating naiveté and idealism. I see them as showing his intuitive business savvy; he began demanding customer service from his staff way before it became a buzz word. It is one of the many positions he has taken that together have enabled the Grameen Bank to prosper for so long.

Yunus observed that transparency and trust are two aspects of management that have always been important to him. "Everybody knows that's why our center meetings are very open meetings, in front of everybody. So when we make payments, it's not inside a side room where you go and do it. You count [the money] in front of everybody. ... And when the staff leaves, before he leaves, the center chief has to sign, 'We have given you so much money in repayment.' All transparent. And then we always say you trust everybody. It's important. But trust has to be backed up by your system. So that it's not broken. It's not misused."[11]

Yunus created an institutional culture that stood in stark contrast to the corruption that was the usual way of doing business in Bangladesh. Staff often repeat a story about him that captures one of his tactics for accomplishing this. When Grameen moved into its offices in Dhaka, Yunus was asked by the phone company for the usual bribe before any additional phones could be installed in the building. He refused, and for week after week Grameen had only a single phone to handle

its business. Whenever people complained about the
lack of phones, Yunus would explain that the phone
company had asked for a bribe and he had refused to pay
it because that would have been dishonest. One day a
top executive from the phone company was at a meeting
where Yunus gave the group the usual explanation about
the phone situation. In a matter of a few hours, the
phones that had been delayed for months were delivered
to the Bank, where they were installed within minutes.[12]

At Grameen, promotions were always announced
in the same month of each year. This procedure was
unlike the more random systems at other Bangladeshi
organizations and meant that Grameen employees always
knew when they would learn whether or not they had
made it to the next grade for the next year, and where
they stood in the organization.

One incentive to keep the staff from dipping into
the till was the Bank's very attractive retirement plan.
After working at the Bank for 10 years, a staff person
could take half the retirement benefit and retire with a
significant sum of money. Yunus told me, "Of course, if
you stole some money, you were immediately fired. You
didn't get any benefit, anything."[13]

Yunus always humored his adversaries. Dowla firmly
believes that this way of dealing with conflict allowed
Yunus to develop the Grameen Bank into an institution
of such stature and importance. He never confronted

anyone. And he expected a lot from his staff. If he
was not pleased with the performance of one of his
employees, he would totally ignore that person—who
usually got the message quickly.

"Simple" is the word Yunus often used to describe the
lifestyle of the staff. Dowla thought it was more accurate
to call it a life of hardship. Staff were not well paid. They
worked in remote areas, often far from their families.
They had to travel by foot or bicycle to attend the center
meetings, through extreme heat in the summer months
and flooding in the rainy season. But Yunus never asked
anyone to work harder than he did, and his salary was
small—ridiculously small, compared to the salaries of
managing directors of other major banks. Even as the
Bank became profitable, his salary remained minimal.
Until 2010, no one ever accused him of taking money
from the Bank for his personal use.

For decades, Yunus made great efforts to hire women,
although it was difficult to find qualified women who
would agree to the lifestyle the Bank demanded. He even
lowered the educational requirements for women. But
few women in this conservative country were prepared
to leave their families and work in the countryside,
which is where all new hires started. Yunus felt strongly
about this, believing that if they hadn't spent time in
the villages, new employees couldn't understand what
Grameen Bank was all about. The fact that the staff has

continued to be overwhelmingly male and the number of women staff has remained so low is one of Yunus's major disappointments. I wonder whether, if he had been more willing to compromise about requiring women to live in remote villages, he might have had more success.

In 1998, the smooth operations of the Grameen Bank were upset by another natural catastrophe, the worst flood in the history of the region. More than two-thirds of Bangladesh was under water for 11 weeks. The Bank declared 42 percent of its centers disasters and suspended all collection of outstanding loans there. Many Grameen borrowers whose homes were destroyed and assets ruined survived by turning to other sources of help, like moneylenders. By 1999, overall repayment rates at Grameen had plummeted and many borrowers stopped coming to the center meetings.

At first everyone assumed that all these problems at the Bank were related to the flood. But soon it became clear that was not the case. Some centers where all the borrowers were up to date in their repayments were close to centers where few of the borrowers were making regular repayments. That meant there must be other factors at work. In fact, the highest ranking managers had gradually come to believe that a complete restructuring of the Bank was necessary. The rigid rules, the one-size-fits-all model that had been so successful for so many years and that had made borrowing easy for illiterate borrowers, was no longer working. These top managers were able to persuade Yunus to accept the fact that a new model must be designed to replace the old one.

Many successful CEOs are not able to adapt to changing circumstances. It says a lot about Yunus that he could listen and could embrace the need for change— and, once convinced, could lead the charge. Furthermore, he was strong enough that he did not allow himself to be pushed aside or sidelined as the Bank was restructured.

Yunus explained to me, "When I started to say, 'Let's do this,' people were shocked. The rank and file staff were shocked. For them, [the old model] was like a religion … I said, 'Look, if I don't do it, nobody ever can do it.' They said, 'No, no, the whole thing will collapse. You do not understand what you're doing. You're too far removed from the reality. You are sitting there in Dhaka.' I said, 'Leave it to me. Let's do it.'"[14]

"It was a very hard process to change the mindset, to change rules, to change processes and so on," Yunus continued.[15] In 1999 the Head Office identified the branches with the worst problems and set up two task forces to get them up and running again as quickly as possible. Yunus delegated to the task forces the power to do whatever they thought was necessary to rehabilitate the centers involved. This approach showed promise right away, and he soon launched another nine task forces.

Dipal Barua, Yunus's long-time golden boy, was the person he had selected to manage the overall change process. As Barua had demonstrated exceptional talent as a manager, Yunus had given him more and more responsibilities. And as usual, he relied on his original group of colleagues from Chittagong to assume the other leadership roles required. Each task force met weekly, and its minutes were circulated to all the other task forces. This enabled everyone to learn from each other's successes, and they were able to make rapid progress in bringing the wayward branches back into the fold.

From this trial and error process, which involved many people at different levels, a gradual consensus emerged for how the new model of Grameen should look. Those on the task forces began to call the original model "classical Grameen" and the new model "Grameen II." The basic difference between them was that Grameen II offered far more flexibility to borrowers than classical Grameen. The incentives supporting joint liability of members of the small groups were dropped. This meant that a group member was no longer expected to bail out another member having trouble keeping up her payments. The Bank now allowed groups to exceed the magic number of five members. All the various kinds of loans that had developed over time—the loans for small businesses, housing, and leasing, as well as seasonal loans and cattle loans—were consolidated into one basic loan. Before this change, a borrower might take out four different kinds of loans at the same time, making tracking of the repayment complicated for both the Bank and the borrower.

Terms of loans could be now adapted to an individual's particular circumstances. For example, a woman might have a loan that needed to be repaid in a year. If her husband died during that year, she could now change the terms of her loan to gain extra time for getting back on her feet. New services such as insurance and a pension fund were introduced, partly as incentives to former borrowers to return to the Bank. There was a new focus on keeping each branch profitable and a move from any dependence on external sources of financing. Most important, perhaps, was the Bank's new emphasis on attracting savings, which could be used to fund more loans. Savings, it was now seen, were a key to sustainability.

Once the basic outlines of Grameen II were in place, the next step was to persuade the 13,000 people on the staff and the 2.4 million borrowers to implement the new ways of working. For this challenging task, Yunus turned once again to Barua. He asked him to lead the new unit charged with writing up Grameen II's rules and regulations and get them implemented. In 2000, all the senior managers of the Bank, including Yunus, attended a workshop to review and finalize the new model. Participants at the workshop made a critical decision—to implement the model slowly, introducing the changes at just one center of each of several branches before moving on to other centers and branches. Gradually, after they had figured out the best ways to actually get borrowers and staff to buy into the new model, they picked up the pace and moved on to more branches. Yunus and Barua toured the countryside to promote Grameen II, often meeting with borrowers and staff from early morning until late into the night, listening to their concerns and talking up the benefits of this new way of working.

Every major organizational transformation is a multi-year process that requires vision and persistence. Employees always resist change and try to hold on to what has worked in the past. What is amazing is that Yunus was able to bring off the organizational transformation successfully. He wisely supported a lengthy planning and gradual implementation process that helped get the staff and borrowers on board. And he created management structures and processes to accomplish the shift. Yunus told me, "People remember to this day what happened between 2000 and 2005 transforming Grameen I to Grameen ll. This is something you remember like the Long March in China."[16]

Believing that the way this change process was managed was significant, Yunus asked Barua and Dowla to document how Grameen II came into being, from start to finish. Barua, of course, had been a major actor on the scene, while Dowla, as an academic, contributed research and writing skills to the project. Barua and Dowla spent many days over the next few years pouring through all the records and writing up how it happened. Their book, *The Poor Always Pay Back: The Grameen II Story*, appeared in 2006.

The more I learned the details of how Yunus led and managed the Grameen Bank, the more I was impressed by the steadiness of his hand on the tiller. By 2010, there were some red flags, however. Yunus was 70 years old, he had not spoken about retiring, and there was no succession plan. Most of the Bank's senior managers had been with him for 30 years. Dowla told me with that he feared Yunus's failure to bring in fresh managerial talent would be his Achilles heel. When Barua left the Bank in 2009, Yunus appointed Nurjahan as Deputy Managing Director. But it was not at all clear that she could bring the kind of leadership the Bank would need in the next decade. She was near retirement age herself. Dowla was uncomfortably aware that the managers had all come from within and were not up to date in use of the latest technology or changing accounting practices. When I was in Bangladesh in 2010, it was uncertain whether Yunus would deal with these issues or not. I was concerned.

*Katharine Esty with Prime Minister
Khaleda Zia in 1995.*

Chapter Nine:

Dealing with Donors

Yunus had actively sought grants and loans from donor agencies and foundations from the days of his earliest projects in the '70s. He continued to be extremely successful at raising money as he struggled to expand the Grameen Bank into more and more locations. Yet today he always makes it sound as though the donors thrust their money at him and he was totally uninterested in it. He may remember that he was reluctant to accept funds, but clearly an important aspect of his success in growing the Grameen Bank was his extraordinary ability to persuade international aid agencies to provide him with millions of dollars. The story of his relations with these donors highlights his unorthodox ways of getting things done and sheds more light on the character of the man.

Before Yunus was even 25, he had demonstrated his flair for business with his packaging company. He had learned how to raise money during his months in Washington in 1971 lobbying for the Bangladeshi cause. He discovered early on, "If you ask for $10,000 or $15,000, donors don't care. If you ask for a million dollars, then it's, 'Let's have lunch.'"[1]

He remembers his initial fundraising in Bangladesh this way: "Our first money came from the International Fund for Agricultural Development, IFAD. I had no idea what they did, who they were. A group of eight or so came and looked at us because someone told them, 'There's a professor working on something in the villages. See if you can help him.' And they spent the whole day. They asked lots of questions. I said, 'We never asked for money from anybody.' They went on, 'We don't think we will recommend you because we don't think what you are doing is really banking.'" Besides, the group told him, they were put off because he was working with the landless poor and so his project had nothing at all to do with agriculture.

A week after that visit, Yunus got a phone call saying that IFAD would like to talk to him again. Their vice president had several million dollars that he needed to spend quickly before he lost them at the end of his budget year, and, besides, he wanted to support Yunus. So the group returned and this time spun arguments about why IFAD should give money to Yunus. "I said 'No,'" he recalls, "but they kept coming back saying, 'Please, take some money.'"[2]

Yunus needed to raise large sums of money because the costs of providing small loans to the poor were far more extensive than the expenses other banks faced. The Grameen Bank had to build a meeting house in each tiny village and then send a staff person to each weekly meeting at that center. The paperwork needed to track the repayment of small loans, as well as the lengthy training process required for each new hire, added to the costs. Yunus knew that he needed additional funds for the start-up phase of each branch but figured that, once a branch was firmly established, it should be able to break even or make money. Before long, he was turning to the international aid agencies for those start-up funds.

The $3.4 million from that first IFAD loan in 1981 gave him a huge boost. He was able to take the Grameen project into five additional districts in Bangladesh. That same year the Ford Foundation provided him with a fund of $800,000 that he could use if he needed it. They had supported his work in rural development in the early '70s, and now they wanted to help him prove to the commercial banks that his model was viable.

By 1982, the IFAD folks were writing enthusiastic reports about Yunus's accomplishments—how he was helping the landless poor and improving the social status of women, too. Word of the Grameen Project spread like wildfire through international aid agencies, which were always on the lookout for promising organizations to fund. Soon these agencies were competing with one another to fund Grameen.

From 1981 until 1995, the Grameen Bank received subsidies, grants, and low interest loans from international donors, some of which were funneled through the Bangladeshi government banks. By 1987 Grameen had received grants for $38 million and Yunus was looking for another $100 million to meet his goal of expanding to 1,000 branches. The grants continued to pour in.

This was the time where there was a rising tide of scathing indictments about the way the international aid agencies and the World Bank operated. Critics, of whom Yunus was one of the most vocal, accused the agencies of loading developing countries with debt and sponsoring projects that didn't really work. They reported how most of the money given by the donor agencies went back to consultants from the donor countries for work on projects that the donors thought were important.

According to James Novak, who wrote a book called *Bangladesh: Reflections on the Water*, it worked like this. If a country has excess capacity in its machine tool industry or wants to get rid of extra machinery, the aid agency will offer to send these items to Bangladesh.[3] The consultants who were sent along to help lived like royalty in the Third World, right next to the heart-rending poverty they were supposedly addressing.

In the spirit of full disclosure, I have to admit that I was one of those development consultants living in luxury whenever I worked in Bangladesh as a consultant on short-term assignments at UNICEF in the 1990s. I stayed at four or five-star hotels and ate food from sumptuous buffets in a country where nearly half of the children were malnourished. And I socialized with these consultants. My friend Kim from Canada, who was on a two-year assignment to UNICEF, lived in a huge house in one of the nice suburbs of Dhaka. On her salary, she could afford a nanny for her four children, two drivers, a cook, a couple of guards, and a man to clean the house. For after work, there was the Canadian Club, where she and her family could play tennis, swim, and relax. For Americans, there was the American Club.

One scene haunts me. Kim and I and several other consultants had gone to a Chinese restaurant for dinner. We couldn't eat all the food that we had ordered, so we asked the waiter to pack up the leftovers. As we emerged from the restaurant, we saw three scrawny little boys playing by the side of the road in the dust. Kim handed them the food. Speaking firmly in Bangla, she directed the boys to share the food among the three of them. They tore open the white cardboard containers with a frightening ferocity, scooping out the food with their hands, and shoving it down their throats in less than a minute. I wept to see how hungry they were.

When I toured one of the show-piece slums that had been improved with a couple of latrines for more than 800 people, I felt sick to my stomach from the smell on the street and shamed by my repulsion. But I soothed my discomfort by thinking, "I am trying to help."

Yunus, by contrast to the international consultants and Bangladeshi businessmen, always lived in a four-room apartment. He had no fancy car, no club, and no second home. He also spoke with passion and fury about the fact that none of the international agencies made alleviating poverty a priority. "After $25 billion you don't see any positive change in Bangladesh. Poverty is wider and deeper." He continued, "The whole country turned into a graveyard of ideas and projects. And each time there's lots of excitement, all the experts saying, 'This is it. You can't go wrong with this.' You go to the graveyard. There are a least 552 projects of the same nature which failed. But nobody talks about them."[4]

Yunus had particular disdain for the World Bank and for years refused to accept any money from them. The World Bank complained that he took money from everybody else but Yunus would not back down. To some observers, he seemed to delight in making a big show of thumbing his nose at the Goliath of development institutions.

"Grameen is nobody's project," he said.[5] He made it clear that any agencies wanting to work with him and Grameen would have to change their ways of doing business. For example, he insisted that people from donor agencies come to his office rather than meeting at theirs. He refused to act subservient or deferential. He told one agency that all the money they spent evaluating whether or not to fund him would have been much better spent if they had just handed it to some poor people.

Donor agencies required detailed reports from the Grameen Bank and all other organizations that received their funds. Yunus realized that if he were to continue to get funded, many of the Bank's systems needed improvement. He turned to his contacts at the Ford Foundation and asked them whether they knew another "crazy banker" who could help him. The people at Ford suggested Mary Houghton and Ron Gryzwinski, two of the co-founders of the South Shore Bank in Chicago, a community development bank with a mission, like Grameen's, to work with poor people.

Houghton and Gryzwinski arrived in Dhaka in 1983 and began a decade-long conversation with Yunus about poverty and banking. Houghton explains that Yunus saw them as like-minded and friendly and he soon came to trust them. This was the first of a dozen or so visits. As they traveled around the countryside with him, they were amazed by all the Bank had accomplished to improve the lives of its borrowers, and also by the way the borrowers treated Yunus—as if he were an emperor or a head of state.

The two found that many Grameen banking practices were inadequate. The Bank's accounting procedures, for example, did not meet accepted international standards.

Yunus's extraordinarily high rate of repayment, over 98 percent, was possible in part because of his unique way of calculating the rate. For example, the Bank provided extra time to borrowers to make up repayments before they were considered delinquent.

With their in-depth knowledge of banking systems, Houghton and Gryzwinski were able to help in various ways, such as developing 10-year projections of the growth of the Grameen Bank. During their many visits to Bangladesh, they tried to act as mediators between Yunus and the donor agencies and to stop him from alienating his benefactors. Houghton understood that Yunus didn't want to be pushed around, why he was quick to get angry, and why he refused to accept this or that. He was a skilled negotiator, and she remembers that it was the donors who usually gave in. The development experts at the international agencies were surprised by his ability to debate and his quick repartees—skills they did not expect to see in a Bangladeshi. But many donors were upset by his behavior, feeling that he was arrogant and hypocritical. He accepted money from the aid agencies and then never expressed gratitude. Worse yet, he often spoke badly of them in public.

Houghton told me, "Yunus, like many entrepreneurs, was certain he was right. He was smart, but the donors became exasperated by his intransigence and, gradually, enraged."[6] She thinks he oversimplified the development

process with his insistence that credit was the key to
everything. "Economic development isn't as simple as he
publicly states." Poor entrepreneurs can't connect with
markets and don't have enough management capacity to
run a larger business. "Of course, before Grameen came
along, no one had figured out how to do credit on a cost-
effective basis at scale."[7] Houghton told me that she and
Gryzwinski have not kept up with Yunus or seen him
since 1993.

Yunus's comments about entrepreneurs do make
economic development sound so simple. He has said, "I
believe that all human being are potential entrepreneurs.
Some of us get the chance to express this talent, but
many of us never get the chance because we were made
to imagine that an entrepreneur is someone enormously
gifted and different from ourselves."[8] He also realized
that there were not enough jobs with salaries and
wages to put everyone in the countryside to work. So
to him, the solution was self-evident: he must get credit
to the rural poor so they could start or improve small
businesses. And he firmly believed that if they had a bit
of money, they could succeed.

In 1993 Yunus made enough peace with the World
Bank to accept $2 million from them. But while he was
in Washington, D.C., that year, he made a speech blasting
the World Bank for its reliance on a rigid theoretical
framework, its narrow focus on financial growth, and,

most of all, for the fact that it did not make the reduction of poverty a top priority. Back in Bangladesh, he went so far as to say Bangladesh would be better off if it had never accepted any foreign aid.

As we have seen, Yunus was not opposed to foreign aid, although this statement certainly sounds like that. This was typical Yunus, driving home his point. As one consultant put it, "But slamming foreign aid in principle when he takes it himself? I find it difficult to stomach."[9] But by the mid '90s, Yunus had come to realize that as long as he kept taking money from donors, no one would believe that his bank could survive without grants and subsidies. And it was obvious that he had not proved that his model of banking was sustainable. By 1994, what he had accomplished was taking his model to scale. The Bank had more than two million borrowers and more than 1,000 branches. And that year it had even made the tiniest sliver of a profit.

Yunus was determined to prove that the Bank could be profitable without grants or loans. In 1995, he announced formally that the Grameen Bank would not accept any more funding from any donor. Some grants were already in process, so subsidies continued to roll in. But he has stuck to that decision and has not accepted any new money from donors since 1995.

In 2010, Yunus told me that the biggest regret of his career is that he accepted that first money from IFAD back in 1981. It seems now that he may actually think that all those subsidies slowed Grameen in its goal of becoming profitable. Or he may just be striking a pose that fits with his more current thinking. My research, with findings well documented by others, shows that between 1982 and 1995 Yunus sought out and relied on money from the international agencies. He could never have taken the Bank to scale without funds from the donors.

Yunus's rants and raves were also well documented and were, I believe, his way of managing these donors and getting them to play the game the way he wanted. He was also trying to transform the status quo. He once said, "If you keep hitting the big wall called the World Bank, maybe it will begin being chipped away, like the Berlin Wall."[10]

The big wall hasn't fallen, but the chipping away has been significant. In recent years, there have been many changes in how the World Bank and the other international aid agencies operate. They seek more input from the developing countries, and these countries have a larger role in decision-making.

I once told Yunus, "I am really impressed by your ability to raise money." He brushed the comment aside with a look of disdain. This is clearly *not* how he wishes to be known. However, I believe it is the key to the success of the Grameen Bank. Most new ventures flounder because they do not have enough resources to expand. It was Yunus's ability to secure a steady stream of funding from the international aid agencies between 1981 and 1995 that enabled him to take his model to scale. And it was this expansion that caught the attention of the world and sparked the spread of microcredit.

Former United States President Bill Clinton has admired Yunus for years.

Chapter Ten:
Entrepreneur Extraordinaire

Yunus has been one of the most successful entrepreneurs of all time. In addition to the legendary Grameen Bank, he has founded more than 55 companies in a wide range of industries. Their activities have received little attention in the press, in stark contrast to the story of the Bank that has been repeated so often. The dozen enterprises that Yunus established during the 1990s include some companies that were amazing successes and some that barely survived. They are important pieces of the Yunus story and shed additional light on his character.

By 1990, Yunus understood that the Grameen Bank was not going to eliminate poverty overnight. He still believed credit was a basic human right and a critical tool in the struggle to end poverty. At the same time, he recognized that the poor had many other pressing needs that were keeping them from escaping the bonds of poverty—needs for medical services, for other kinds of financial services, and for assistance in educating their children.

During the 1990s, he set out to create new Grameen companies to address these needs, and by the end of the decade he had established a dozen new entities. All these companies have as their mission the alleviation of poverty. They provide products, services, and jobs for the poor in the areas of health care, banking, food, education, energy, telecommunications, and business. Most of them are not-for-profits and three are for-profits. All are independent of the Grameen Bank.

The managing directors of all these organizations are people whom Yunus trusts and has put in place. He serves as chair of the board for most of these organizations, and the other board members are a reshuffling of the colleagues that have been with him since the beginning. While he is not involved in the day-to-day running of these companies, much of Yunus's time is spent at board meetings thinking through their strategies for the future.

Four of these companies have fared particularly well. Today Grameen Shakti (Energy) is the largest alternative energy company in Bangladesh, GrameenPhone is the largest mobile phone company, Grameen Telecom is the largest mobile virtual network operator, and Grameen Kalyan (Welfare) is the largest healthcare and insurance provider. An astounding accomplishment for one man.

When Yunus established Grameen Shakti (Energy) in 1996 to promote and popularize renewable energy technologies in rural areas of Bangladesh, there was a total lack of awareness of solar energy among the general population, costs were high, and knowledge of the technology was minimal. Yunus placed the always-competent Dipal Barua as managing director of the start-up and counted on him to figure out how to move ahead. Barua trained the staff to go door-to-door to demonstrate the benefits of solar and win the trust of the local people.

Most women in rural Bangladesh use traditional stoves that burn wood and grasses, stoves that capture only 5 to 15 percent of the heat that is produced and emit poisonous fumes that pollute the environment. Grameen Shakti builds bio-gas plants that convert cow dung and poultry wastes into gas for clean cooking in improved stoves. Of course, at first women in the villages resisted the new-fangled stoves, and again the Shakti engineers had to go door to door to persuade women to try them.

Despite all the challenges, the organization flourished. Over the next 14 years, Barua was awarded a number of international prizes for Grameen Shakti's achievements. In 2010, however, Yunus removed Barua from his position as managing director of Grameen Shakti and as number two at the Grameen Bank. When I asked Yunus what had happened, he explained without emotion that Barua had stopped being loyal to him. He refused to take direction from Yunus anymore, and he let it be known that it was time for Yunus to step down from the Bank. But Yunus wasn't ready for retirement. Their relationship ended abruptly and the rupture was total.

Twenty-Seven Dollars and a Dream

Asif Dowla, who co-authored with Barua the book *The Poor Always Pay Back: The Grameen II Story*, remains devoted to both Yunus and Dipal Barua. He has been terribly saddened about the end of their 35-year relationship. On the other hand, as I have said, Yunus has seemed somewhat matter-of-fact about it. At the time, I was a little nonplussed by this reaction. With more thought, it dawned on me that this lack of emotion may be part of the toolkit of the successful entrepreneur. In any case, it is Yunus's way of operating to keep moving ahead and to avoid dwelling on failures and broken relationships.

Today there is a new managing director of Grameen Shakti and the organization now has more than 5,000 staff. They have installed more than 250,000 solar home systems, developed 7,000 bio-gas plants, and placed thousands of improved stoves in village homes. They hope to break even in the near future.

GrameenPhone, unlike Grameen Shakti, is a for-profit company that has been a commercial success for years. It is now the largest tax payer in Bangladesh. GrameenPhone was the brainchild of a Bangladeshi named Iqbal Quadir who had been trained at the Wharton School of Business at the University of Pennsylvania. The idea for a company came to him as he remembered an incident from his childhood.

Quadir had been sent to a town miles away from his home to get medicine for a sick family member. After walking for four hours he arrived at the town only to find that the pharmacist was away. As an adult, Quadir began to mull over the real cost of this lack of communication in Bangladesh and started to gather data. He learned that at that time, 1993, Bangladesh had only two phones per 1,000 people and that almost all of these phones were located in cities. And at that time in Bangladesh, a cell phone cost $2,000.

Quadir saw the huge potential for cell phones to transform rural Bangladesh. He approached Yunus with his idea, but Yunus wasn't interested. Quadir came back a second time and made a more effective pitch. Famously, he said to Yunus that, since the Grameen Bank makes loans to women to buy cows so they can improve their income, "Why can't a cell phone be like a cow?" By 1994, Yunus was on board with the idea; but getting the funding for the cell phone initiative proved to be a complicated and drawn-out process.

After months of searching for backers for his idea, Quadir was able to put together a joint venture whose investors included himself, a Norwegian company called Telenor, and Grameen Telecom, a not-for-profit organization. Telenor had the majority interest and Grameen Telecom had a 28 percent interest, while Quadir owned less than 5 percent. The plan was that

GrameenPhone would secure the cellular license and operate the network. Grameen Telecom would purchase minutes from GrameenPhone and sell them to rural entrepreneurs at below-market rates.

But it was not that easy. The government refused to let the cell phones connect into existing landlines. So Grameen Telecom had to develop their network with cell phones connecting only to other cell phones. At the time, everyone at Grameen continued to doubt whether this would be workable. In 1995, Khalid Shams, then the deputy managing director to the Grameen Bank said that Quadir was very persistent. He was someone who could do the bulldozing.[1] And after many false starts and several years of work by Quadir, it all came together.

Today GrameenPhone is the leading cellular telephone service provider in Bangladesh with more than 32 million subscribers. As the company became profitable, Quadir grew unhappy with the tiny proportion of the profits he received after having done so much of the work. The relationship between him and Yunus, which had once been close, deteriorated. Yunus explained to me that Quadir claims too much credit for the success of Grameen Phone and never acknowledges the contributions that Yunus made to the company.[2] Quadir is presently the director of the Legatum Institute for Development and Entrepreneurship at MIT and is known as a global leader in providing telephone services in the developing world.

When I asked Yunus about Quadir, I would have liked him to be a little more self-reflective and forthcoming about their relationship. I was reminded of how he brushed off my questions about Dipal Barua. I know that entrepreneurs are generally thick-skinned. Still, I wondered whether Yunus's stiff upper lip approach and his "Let's just move on" attitude reflect his years of training in the Boy Scouts, his reliance on an inner spirituality, or just his focus on mission. I went with the mission.

The meteoric rise of the Village Phone Program, developed under the wing of Grameen Telecom, is one of the most amazing stories of Yunus's entrepreneurial ventures. It was this program that transformed Quadir's vision of the cell phone as a cash cow into a reality. A woman who wanted to be part of the Village Phone Program bought a cell phone with money she acquired from a loan from the Grameen Bank. After a month or so of training, she was ready for business. Customers came to the home of the "telephone lady" to make a call.

Yunus had arranged that a woman named Laily Begum would make the first phone call—to Prime Minister Sheikh Hasina, with whom Yunus was always careful to share some of the limelight. So it was that in March of 1997, with a crowd watching, Laily—an illiterate woman living in a small village—dialed up the prime minister for a chat. In the next few hours, a dozen people in the village placed calls though Laily and her business was launched.

It turned out there was a huge need for these cell phone services—to reach distant family members, for business, and for medical assistance. The number of telephone ladies grew faster than anyone had anticipated. By 2006 there were about 250,000 women providing phone service to 55,000 villages. It would have taken decades for landlines and electricity to reach the remote villages where these women set up their businesses. By going directly to cell phones, the program leapfrogged over the use of landlines and skipped a whole stage of technical development.

Over the next decade, cell phones became so common in Bangladesh that the businesses became a victim of progress. The Village Phone Program withered away almost as quickly as it had sprung up. In a 2007 interview appearing in *Fast Company*, Laily reported, "Hardly anyone uses my phone anymore." But in 1997, Laily had lived in a mud house. By 2007, she had a brick house with four rooms, and a second house. She could afford to send her children to school. In 2010, her net worth was $145,000 and she was the richest person in her village.[3]

Not all of Yunus's companies have been success stories. Grameen Uddog, for example, has been grappling with a series of challenges ever since its beginning in

1993. Yunus and his colleague and old friend Khalid Shams founded Grameen Uddog hoping to revive the moribund textile industry that had once played a central role in the local economy. Among Uddog's products is a brand of hand-woven plaid fabrics called Grameen Check. Yunus wants to make wearing Grameen Check an act of national pride, particularly among the men pulling rickshaws who by tradition wear a skirt-like garment called a lunghi. He himself always wears a shirt or tunic that is made of material that has been hand-woven in Bangladesh.

Grameen Uddog has encountered roadblocks. Hand-woven material is always pricier than machine-made, and neither wholesalers nor the unions cooperated with the new company. In addition, it was difficult to get their products to international markets. While in the last four years Grameen Uddog has exported more than 15 million yards of fabric to Europe and the United States, and while every rickshaw puller I saw in Bangladesh appeared to be sporting Grameen Check, the future remains uncertain.

Yunus's almost unlimited faith in the potential of all people to become successful entrepreneurs has led him to test this belief with his Struggling Members Program. This program attempts to turn beggars, the most downtrodden of all the poor in Bangladesh, into small business owners and entrepreneurs. The Grameen Bank lends tiny amounts of money to these impoverished people even though they are too poor to qualify for loans, even from Grameen. The loans are offered interest-free and are typically as small as $10. The beggars typically use their loans to buy sundries like snacks, candy, pickles, and cosmetics that they can sell in their villages for a small profit. The Bank encourages its staff members to individually mentor these struggling members.

The major problem mentors report is the mindset of the beggars who find it hard to believe they can actually change their lives. In 2005, when there were about 66,000 members in the program, 786 had given up begging. By 2010 the Struggling Member Program had reached 112,000 members, but the number who had actually given up begging remained small.

To get the inside story of Yunus as entrepreneur, I turned to Vidar Jorgensen, a hugely successful entrepreneur himself, who now donates 60 percent of his time to working with Yunus. Jorgensen is the majority owner of seven healthcare conference and research companies, which own and manage more than 300 conferences and several membership-based research groups. One of his companies is the World HealthCare Congress, which was launched in conjunction with the *Wall Street Journal* and CNBC.

"Yunus, of course, is the classic entrepreneur," Jorgensen said as we sat on the front porch of the Colonial Inn in Concord, Massachusetts, our shared hometown. He continued, "Yunus is a glass-half-filled kind of person. He is always optimistic and he doesn't get rattled by failure. It's hard not to like him. Yunus is not afraid of change or trying new things. Many people think it is easy to start a new company, like starting a restaurant. Everyone thinks they can start a restaurant. But it is harder than it looks and 50 percent of them fail in the first year. Yunus has started over 25 companies."[4]

Jorgensen first met him in 1993 when Yunus attended one of Jorgensen's conferences on healthcare economics. Jorgensen was intrigued by Yunus's ideas of bottom-up economics and bottom-up change, and was inspired by his vision of alleviating poverty. Further, he saw that Yunus had an approach that was both practical and successful. "His ideas matched my own," is how he put it. Soon Jorgensen was actually working with Yunus, taking no compensation for his many hours and paying for his own travel. In 2012 he spent much of his time finding resources for Yunus's healthcare company in Bangladesh, Grameen Kalyan. Grameen Kalyan provides healthcare services to poor rural families at 53 centers that focus on early detection and prevention as well as basic clinical services.[5]

Unlike Yunus, Jorgensen keeps a low profile, and his activities rarely make the news. I told him I thought he was unique and interesting—a super-entrepreneur donating 60 percent of his time as a volunteer in support of another entrepreneur. His response was that he was just one of 50 or so business partners who have been drawn to Yunus and his mission. And turning the attention away from himself, he began listing names of others who are devoting major parts of their lives to Yunus's dream.

Jorgensen is also the main fundraiser for Grameen America, Yunus's most recent effort to demonstrate that microcredit programs can work in the U.S.A. More about that in the next chapter.

Successful entrepreneurs never stop generating new ideas. And so it has been with Yunus. Since 2006, Yunus has been focusing much of his energy on social business—launching a host of new ventures in Bangladesh and around the globe. But that, too, is a story for a later chapter.

The Grameen Family of Organizations – a partial list

Grameen Trust, 1989, providing support to replications of the Grameen Bank around the world.

Grameen Krishi (Agriculture), 1991, a for-profit company that lends money to farmers who are poor but not the poorest of the poor.

Grameen Uddog, 1993, a not-for-profit company that works with 10,000 hand-loom weavers and organizes them into an export business.

Grameen Fund, 1994, a not-for-profit company that provides financing to poor entrepreneurs for ventures that, while risky, promise good return.

Grameen Shikkha (Education), 1994, a not-for-profit company that promotes mass education in rural area by providing financial support such as loans and grants and by conducting programs such as an Early Childhood Development Program.

Grameen Fish and Livestock, 1994, a not-for-profit company that operates fish farms, shrimp farms, and fish seed farms.

Grameen Telecom, 1995, a not-for-profit company that owns a partial stake in GrameenPhone. It provides mobile phones to the villages of Bangladesh and is the nation's largest mobile network operator.

Grameen Shamogee (Products), 1996, a for-profit company that finances rural industries and helps market their products, such as traditional Bangladeshi crafts.

Grameen Cybernet, 1996, a for-profit company dedicated to bringing the latest in information technology, including the internet, to Bangladesh. It is the nation's largest internet service provider.

Grameen Shakti, 1996, a not-for-profit company that aims to develop non-polluting renewable energy, including solar, bio-gas, and wind turbines, in rural villages.

GrameenPhone, 1996, the leading telecommunications provider in Bangladesh, with more than 50 percent of the Bangladeshi market. In 2011 it had more than 32 million subscribers. It is a for-profit joint venture enterprise between Telenor and Grameen Telecom.

Grameen Kalyan (Healthcare), 1996, a not-for-profit company that provides health services to the rural poor. It has established 53 clinics with community health outreach and emergency services, as well as micro health-insurance programs.

Grameen Communications, 1997, a not-for-profit company that aims to increase awareness of information on the internet to improve education, health, and sanitation.

Grameen Solutions, the flagship technology company within the Grameen family of organizations. Services offered include website design, software solutions, and IT solutions.

Grameen Byabosa Bikash (Grameen Business Promotions), 2001, providing marketing, technical, and financial support to rural entrepreneurs.

Yunus with Afrosi, his wife, his father, and daughter Deena.

Chapter Eleven:

Going to the Moon

The Microcredit Summit of 1997 was the moment when the world took note of microcredit and its power to help the poor. It was also a tipping point for the influence of Muhammad Yunus. And it was the point at which microcredit became a world movement that within 10 years would reach 100 million of the earth's poorest people.

Yunus electrified the participants at the Microcredit Summit held in Washington, D.C., in 1997, when he spoke these words:"Only sixty-five years after the twelve-second flight of the Wright brothers, man went to the moon. Sixty-five years after this summit, we will also go to our moon. We will create a poverty-free world."[1]

During the decade before the Microcredit Summit, a number of people had established replications of the Grameen Bank in Malaysia, the Philippines, India, Nepal, Vietnam, China, Latin America, and Africa. These replications tried to import the essential Grameen, a set of interrelated practices and principles, in order to provide credit to those at the bottom rung of the economic pyramid. In each of these different countries and cultures, the replications took hold. Poor women everywhere, it seemed, want to create a better life for themselves and their children. The Grameen model found a way to tap into this universal desire. Helen Todd, who edited the book *Cloning Grameen Bank*, wrote, "This almost primordial drive fuels the replications of the Grameen Bank model."[2]

The founding leaders of these replications faced enormous difficulties. Almost all of them got off to a good start. However, most of them found it difficult to expand their programs and to significantly increase the number of their borrowers. The major reason was a shortage of funds. Resources in the form of grants or loans from the outside were needed to open up new branches, build new centers, and train new staff. After all, it had taken Yunus 17 years to reach the point where the Grameen Bank was profitable. The donor agencies that had helped him launch the Bank showed little interest in replication projects. It seemed that skilled fundraisers and charismatic spokespersons were needed to persuade donors to get involved with these outposts of Grameen.

When Yunus became aware of the difficulties that the replications were facing, being an inveterate problem solver, he soon came up with ways to help. In 1989, he established the Grameen Trust, located in Dhaka, to secure additional funding for these projects. Now the funds flowed; the MacArthur Foundation, followed by the Rockefeller Foundation, the World Bank, the U.S. government, and the German government provided grants to the Grameen Trust, which in turn channeled the funds to replications in the four corners of the world.

Yunus was convinced that those replicators who stuck close to the Grameen model would have far fewer problems than those who strayed away from the core principles. Once or twice a year, the Grameen Bank and the Grameen Trust offered a program to train potential replicators from around the world. During part of the two-week session, participants lived in a village and observed several branches of the Bank in action. They also interviewed individual borrowers at great length in order to deepen their understanding of the mindset of a poor person. Yunus insisted that a commitment to helping the poorest of the poor was an essential part of the model. He still had faith that once potential replicators understood even one very poor person, they would see the enormous skills the poor were already using just to survive and would come to believe in their potential to run small businesses.

There have been many attempts to bring microcredit to the U.S.A. In 1985 Yunus came to this country at the invitation of Mary Houghton, his former consultant from the ShoreBank, to explore the possibility of a replication of the Grameen Bank in Chicago. Although Yunus's banking experience was limited to rural regions of Bangladesh, he was not one to be held back by something as inconsequential as inexperience. He soon discovered, not surprisingly, that most business people he met in the States were not only skeptical about his idea of small loans to the poorest but also firmly opposed to lending money to poor people. They told him that poor people needed social services, not capital. After some time, Mary Houghton and several colleagues were able to establish the Women's Self-Employment Project—but growing the organization proved to be difficult.

In 1986, Yunus met with Bill and Hillary Clinton in Arkansas to discuss creating a replication there. They arranged a number of meetings for him with small business owners, but he quickly became frustrated because the people he was meeting were not poor. He insisted on meeting with some unemployed people and welfare recipients.

Meeting with these people was also challenging. As Yunus explained his model to this group, they looked at him with blank stares. They told him that no bank would lend money to people like them and it wasn't even worth talking about. Yunus kept asking, "But what if someone would lend you money?" He explained, "I just had a meeting with Governor Clinton and he asked me to bring my bank to your country." Finally a woman piped up, saying that she would like to have a loan of $375 for some supplies for her cosmetic business. And that was the beginning of a Grameen replication called the Good Faith Fund.[3]

By 1997, there were many other microcredit institutions in the United States. Some were replications of the Grameen Bank; others were based on different models. Many of these programs struggled for years and were never able to attract enough borrowers to get anywhere near the break-even point or profitability. Most of the surviving organizations served fewer than 50 clients. Eventually the Women's Self-Employment Project shifted its focus to training women to run home-based day care, while the Good Faith Fund began lending larger amounts of money to small and medium-sized businesses.

What explains the failure to thrive of these microcredit organizations? Some experts point to the fact that there are many fewer opportunities for solo entrepreneurs in America than in developing countries, where they make up a far larger percentage of jobs. Most people in the U.S. work for wages in factories or businesses. Other experts look at the high cost of starting a new business in a country like the United States.

Yunus continued to believe the key problems of replications in the States has stemmed from their lack of rigor in applying the Grameen model. He also continued to believe there is a need in the States because 40 million adults are unbanked, meaning they are not able to use the services of a bank; and he now has the support of his stalwart entrepreneurial friend Vidar Jorgensen. As the most recent of Yunus's U.S. enterprises, Grameen America was launched in Queens, NY, in January 2008, with Jorgensen as its primary fundraiser. Grameen America is staffed with experienced Grameen managers from Bangladesh. Yunus is not taking any chances this time.

Jorgensen has raised enough money so that as of April, 2012, there were seven branches scattered across the country and 9,000 borrowers who have been lent a total of 38 million dollars. With the Jorgensen/Yunus duo behind this project, more expansion and success seem likely.

* * * * *

As microcredit was spreading to every corner of the world with varying degrees of success, John Hatch came up with the idea of bringing replicators together for a conference. Hatch was the founder of FINCA, a U.S.-based microcredit organization that works primarily in Latin America. He and Yunus were both on the board of RESULTS, Sam Daley-Harris's tiny, grassroots citizens' lobbying organization in Washington. The Microcredit Summit of 1997 was put together by these three dynamic visionaries—Yunus, Sam Daley-Harris, and John Hatch.

Hatch's organization, FINCA, like the Grameen Bank, provides small loans to poor working women. Hatch had been completely unaware of Yunus and the Grameen

Bank when he created his model of "village banking."
In his program, village elders create groups of 25 poor
women to receive small loans to grow or start small
businesses.

In 1995 Hatch came up with the idea of setting a
goal for microcredit to reach 200 million of the world's
poorest people with small loans in ten years. He had
been lying in bed recuperating from an illness when the
idea came to him. He wrote a six-page paper explaining
the goal idea, and also the idea of a big conference, a
microcredit summit, to get buy-in for the goal.

Hatch showed the paper to Daley-Harris, and the two
of them passed it on to Yunus. Yunus was excited; he
realized the transformative possibilities of setting such a
bold goal but he believed a target of 100 million people
would be better. He argued that they could actually
reach that goal and that it was still audacious. Fewer
than eight million people worldwide had been reached
by microcredit by 1994, and the three of them would
be aiming to increase that number to 100 million of the
world's poorest people in a mere 10 years.

Hatch is a large and gregarious man in his seventies.
When I met him, in 2011, I asked about his relationship
to Yunus, and he described it this way. "I felt like I was
a brother. I am a hugger, and I feel I Latinized him.
Whenever I met him I would hug him and lift him
right off the ground. He was always surprised and very

gracious." And he added, a bit wistfully, "I put him on our FINCA board, but he never made a meeting. But just having him on our board lent us some of his prestige."[4] No wonder he never made a meeting, I thought to myself. Yunus was managing director of the Grameen Bank and chairman of the board of 20 or so other Grameen organizations.

Sam Daley-Harris, the real mover and shaker behind the Microcredit Summit, was a former percussionist in the Miami Symphony until he became active in the world hunger movement. Convinced of the possibility of ending hunger, he had founded RESULTS to create the political will to actually do it. In its early years, RESULTS held hundreds of press conferences as well as sponsoring forums and conferences to educate the public about ending hunger and poverty. Daley-Harris demonstrated an amazing talent for organizing and for creating big events. In 1990, to publicize the UN Children's Summit, he set up 1,500 candlelight vigils in locations around the world. More than a million people attended these vigils—an amazing feat for that time before email.

Yunus first met Daley-Harris in 1986. Yunus had come to Washington to testify before a congressional subcommittee and the Committee on Hunger. Daley-Harris arranged for Yunus to have two teleconferences with 28 newspaper editors from around the nation. In 2011, Daley-Harris recalled, "Yunus stepped into the

room and was a breath of fresh air."[5] The editor from
the *Christian Science Monitor*, Kristin Helmore, was so
taken by Yunus during the first teleconference that she
asked whether she could stay on for the second one. In
the following days there was a blitz of editorials around
the country and the buzz about Yunus and the Grameen
Bank began to grow.

Kristin Helmore wrote a four-part series about
microcredit and Yunus. It was this series that led CBS to
create a segment about him for *60 Minutes*. This twelve-
minute piece, extracted from hundreds of hours of
filming on site in Bangladesh, was powerful and inspiring.
It enabled the story of how Yunus and the Grameen
Bank were improving the lives of the poorest women in
Bangladesh to reach an audience of millions.

Daley-Harris, Hatch, and Yunus met in Rome to
develop their ideas for the Summit. At first they were
thinking of a conference of maybe 500 people. They
formed the Microcredit Summit Organizing Committee,
which included, among others, representatives from the
World Bank, the Carter Center, and Citicorp. As they
planned, they built upon the processes and traditions of
UN summits—the Children's Summit of 1990, the Earth
Summit of 1992, the Housing Summit in 1996, and the
Women's Conference in Beijing in 1995.

This summit, they decided, would be different from

all the earlier ones. It would be organized by citizens rather than the UN or a government. Its impact would be different, too. They had seen the typical UN conferences where thousands of participants debated for days and the end product was a Declaration and a Plan of Action that outlined some goals and suggestions for action. Then after the summit, nothing happened.

Yunus and the Organizing Committee wanted to go into the Microcredit Summit with the goal already agreed upon, with the word-smithing complete. This turned out to be much harder than they had anticipated. Yunus recalled, "Preparation of a draft declaration proved to be a real hornet's nest. Sam became extremely disappointed. I tried to cheer him up by saying that we had to confront all our academic, institutional, and philosophical differences. It was easy for me to say this and disappear into safety in Dhaka."[6] In fact, it was Daley-Harris, the main organizer of the event, who had to deal with the relentless quibbling and the squabbling.

At the two preparatory conferences that Daley-Harris set up, the process was messy and contentious. After months of work, the planners managed to agree on four core themes for the Summit: reaching the poorest, reaching and empowering women, building financially self-sufficient institutions, and ensuring a positive, measurable impact on the lives of clients and their families. But each agreement had taken hours of discussion and debate.

Some in the field opposed "reaching the poorest" on grounds that it was too costly, and wanted to settle for "reaching the poor." Others challenged "positive impact," insisting that small loans can easily become a burden to the very poor. Some wanted to use the term microfinance rather than microcredit. Microfinance, a broader term, included financial services such as savings as well as lending, and it was preferred by some of the newer, larger organizations whose models differed from the Grameen model. Yunus fought hard and eloquently to stay with term microcredit, which for him signaled an important commitment to the poorest of the poor. His view prevailed after much controversy.

At the end of the planning, the goal of reaching 100 million of the world's poorest families with small loans and other financial and business services by the year 2005 was confirmed.

Yunus already had, by 1997, a following among influential people all over the world, and he was able to attract them to the Summit. He had met dozens of members of Congress and other government officials through Daley-Harris and RESULTS. According to Daley-Harris, Yunus was the lure to get these people to attend the Summit. Yunus was, in fact, the main story.

The Microcredit Summit of 1997 was a triumph, a tour de force that exceeded Yunus's most optimistic hopes for the event. Almost 3,000 participants attended the Summit, which was held in February in Washington, D.C. First Lady Hillary Clinton commented, "I am thrilled to see such a turnout for this Summit, which is one of the most important gatherings that we could have anywhere in our world."[7] It brought together practitioners, donors, representatives from international financial institutions and non-governmental organizations, academics, and government officials involved with microcredit. The luminaries who attended were an impressive group: U.S. Secretary of the Treasury Robert Rubin, the president of the World Bank, and the heads of a half dozen UN agencies. Also present were the queens of Spain and Belgium, the prime ministers of Bangladesh and Mozambique, and the presidents of Mali, Uganda, and Peru.

As Yunus had hoped, the goal was adopted at the first plenary session, enabling the rest of the conference to focus on its implementation. He had been adamant that the voices of the poorest needed to be heard and their presence felt. This was accomplished by kicking off each of the five plenary sessions with a five-minute video of a different borrower from a far-flung region of the world.

When it came time for Yunus to speak, he said, "To me, this summit is a grand celebration—we are celebrating the freeing of credit from the bondage of collateral. This summit pronounces good-bye to a long era of financial apartheid. This summit declares that credit is more than business. Just like food, credit is a human right. ... This summit is about setting the stage to unleash the human creativity and potential of the poor. ... This Summit is to celebrate the success of millions of determined women who transformed their lives from extreme poverty to dignified self-sufficiency through microcredit programs. ... This Summit wants to build will, wants to build capacity, wants to end poverty in the world."[8]

As the Summit came to an end, Daley-Harris announced the formation of the Microcredit Summit Campaign under his leadership at RESULTS. The Campaign would carry on the work accomplished at the Summit and track progress in the future. It would advance the microfinance field and foster a productive learning community. What was particularly unique about the Campaign was its citizen-led approach of establishing and meeting a global goal.

After the Summit, Yunus played a critical role in continuing to build interest in the Microcredit Campaign. John Hatch told me, "Yunus was a fantastic salesman of microcredit. He could have an audience believing in the inevitability of ending poverty in a matter of minutes. He got right to their hearts. He also was crucial in getting huge organizations to imitate the Grameen Bank." But Hatch also added gently, "Perhaps Yunus was too rigid about presenting his model as the best. I see we have a big tent with room for many different models."[9]

To help reach the goal of the Summit, Yunus provided Alex Counts, who had worked closely with him in Bangladesh, with seed money to establish the Grameen Foundation. Its mission is to support existing microfinance organizations and help them grow. Counts shares Yunus's vision and his commitment to extend credit to the poorest of the poor. The Foundation also provides technology assistance, training, and information services to a network of institutions.

In the next decade, microcredit institutions expanded rapidly, reaching almost every country in the world. Microcredit became increasingly accepted as an effective strategy for the alleviation of poverty. Each year, Daley-Harris and the Microcredit Summit Campaign asked every microcredit organization to submit data about the number of clients it had served that year and its action plan. After a few years, the Campaign also asked each one to have its data verified by an outside organization. They wanted solid data to track progress to their goal.

In 2005, more than 3,000 microcredit institutions submitted their data; and at the Microcredit Summit held that year, the Campaign announced that it was very close to meeting its goal. The UN designated 2005 as the Year of Microcredit, recognizing the significance of the movement.

In 2006, the Campaign was able to announce that

it had reached its original goal. The impossible dream was now a reality. When the Campaign began, only 7.6 million families in the world had received microcredit. By 2006, microcredit had reached more than 100 million of the poorest families. What in 1997 had seemed like reaching for the stars had been accomplished. As a result of consistent and rigorous tracking over the years, the Campaign actually knew what progress had been achieved. This was rare for organizations in the international development field.

As their success became evident, in 2005 the Campaign set new goals and raised their sights even higher: "To ensure that 175 million of the world's poorest families, especially the women of those families, are receiving credit for self-employment and other financial and business services by the end of 2015." A second new goal was to ensure that 100 million families rise out of poverty—that is, reach the standard of having more than one U.S. dollar per person per day to live on. The third new goal, one of the UN's Millennium Development Goals, was to cut absolute poverty in half by 2015.

The potential of microcredit had begun to intrigue other movers and shakers. In 2004, the Grameen Foundation organized a weekend seminar on microcredit and invited two dozen wealthy people in the Silicon Valley including Pierre Omidyar, the pony-tailed founder of eBay. Omidyar had become fascinated by microcredit as a powerful tool, a tool that he came to believe could change the world. Those attending the seminar included a number of billionaires, such as the co-founders of Google.

At one point during the weekend, participants were charged with the task of taking the next 45 minutes to come up with ways to end world poverty. Alex Counts reported later, "They were all rushing up taking turns at the white-board. And they took it so seriously!" The event was not a fundraiser. But one of the staff from the Grameen Foundation sensed the energy in the group and their desire for action. He proposed that the participants create a fund by each pledging one-tenth of one percent of their net worth. The fund would be used to guarantee loans that commercial banks made to microfinance institutions. Counts estimated the net worth in the room at about $30 billion. Omidyar got up and wrote on the flip chart, "END WORLD POVERTY NOW."[10]

Several people in the group made pledges right on the spot. Others said they needed a bit more time but indicated they would pledge in a few weeks. As the session came to a close, Yunus was asked how he felt. He replied, "I feel that today was the most important day of my life."[11]

This day was important to Yunus because it was probably the closest he would ever feel to achieving his goal of ending poverty in his lifetime. That day he could almost touch his moon. The promises from those in that room in San Francisco made it seem possible, probable.

By October of 2005, over $31 million had been pledged to the fund and almost all of it was supporting loans to microcredit institutions. By 2006, however, Omidyar's interest had shifted. He summarized his position this way. "For us it's not just about alleviating poverty, it's about economic self-empowerment." His focus became helping microfinance institutions become profitable, become sustainable—while Yunus remained focused on eradicating poverty. Omidyar made a gift of $100 million to Tufts University on condition that it be used to promote the commercialization of microcredit. It is interesting that Omidyar had never visited a microcredit program. This is so different from Yunus, who had devised his model from years spent in the villages observing what worked with poor people and what did not.

Hatch recalls, "The movement split almost before it got started... [It] became bifocal. There were those determined to bring the poorest out of poverty and those who were more interested in the financial success of microfinance organizations." Yunus never wavered from his commitment to the poorest of the poor or from his belief that his model was the best way to get there. But the conviction that he was about to walk on his moon

Lamiya's assistant at the Yunus Centre, Shiban, samples the Grameen Danone yogurt.

Chapter Twelve:

The Next Big Idea

Yunus loves to talk about social business. Usually his first example is Grameen Danone, which is a partnership between the Grameen Bank and a French company, Groupe Danone (Dannon Yogurt in the U.S.). In 2005 Yunus was asked to lunch in Paris with Franck Riboud, the chief executive of Groupe Danone. Riboud, who had worked for a year as a volunteer in a shantytown north of Delhi, told him, "We would like to find a way to help the poor."[1]

Yunus suggested they form a joint venture to provide healthy food for malnourished children in Bangladesh. With little more conversation, Yunus and Riboud shook hands and made a deal. Then Yunus went on to explain that it would be a "social business"—meaning there would be no dividends and all the profits would stay in the business. Riboud agreed.

A few months later, Riboud and a group of his colleagues went to Bangladesh to flesh out the concept for their yogurt. It would be fortified with nutrients—like iron, vitamin A, calcium, zinc, and iodine—that are often lacking in Bangladeshi children's diet. In 2005 almost 40 percent of children in Bangladesh were malnourished, and their growth was often stunted.

At first Yunus thought the French team working on the project was too academic because they insisted on all sorts of analyses. They spent time exploring alternative ways to distribute the yogurt in the steamy, hot climate of rural Bangladesh where people had no refrigerators, and how to give the yogurt a good taste in spite of the added nutrients. Yunus was impatient to get going. He was used to charging ahead with his ideas, trusting his intuition. But he came to see that, as they gathered more data, the product improved.

The new venture faced numerous challenges, some of which were imposed by Yunus himself. Although Groupe Danone was used to building one large central plant when they expanded into a new country, he insisted they build a small factory out in the countryside in order to benefit the people living there. He was also vehement that the price of their yogurt had to be affordable for poor people—five takas, now worth about seven cents per cup.

Because of Yunus's experience with the Grameen phone ladies, the Grameen Danone managers decided to hire village women to sell their yogurt. They were disappointed when most of the women quit after a day or two on the job. Danone managers came to understand that selling door to door was just not culturally acceptable. The phone ladies had worked primarily from their homes. With a new process that involved many of the husbands and more extensive training, the company was able to grow the number of saleswomen, but they never achieved anything like the success that had been achieved with the phone ladies.

After they got started, Grameen Danone found it needed to tweak their recipe for yogurt, adding a bit more sweetening to increase its appeal to children. Now its molasses flavor tastes good, to adults, too. I can vouch for that.

Then another challenge. Food prices began to rise around the world in 2006 and 2007, and before long the price of milk in Bangladesh had doubled. It was apparent to Yunus that despite his insistence on keeping the product affordable, Grameen Danone would have to raise its prices to become sustainable. And as he feared, when the price of a cup went from five takas to eight takas, the results were catastrophic. Sales dropped about 80 percent, and the number of saleswomen plummeted once again. It took another few years to get back on track. In 2012, Yunus was still convinced that the company was just about to hit the breakeven point.

Grameen Veolia Water, a venture with another French multinational company, was Yunus's second major attempt to create a social business in Bangladesh. Like Grameen Danone, it had difficulties getting started. In

1993, it had been discovered that much of the water in Bangladesh was contaminated by naturally formed arsenic carried down from the Himalayas in the rivers. Over the long term, arsenic causes health problem like skin lesions and cancer. It was estimated that between 30 and 80 million people living in rural Bangladesh were drinking this polluted water.

Yunus understood the mindset of the villagers and foresaw that the poor would not buy water unless it was very, very cheap, like one taka—less than two cents—for about three gallons. He was afraid that this low price would not be feasible. But the engineers from Veolia were determined to do it and the managers, too, were totally behind this pilot project.

Yunus has always believed in starting small, so the team chose the small village of Goalmari, about 30 miles from Dhaka, for a first site. Benoit Ringot, the current project manager, told me that Yunus was eager to move quickly:"He was very pushy, very involved, very supportive, even when things did not work out as we hoped."[2]

The engineers decided to use water from the nearby river rather than creating wells, and to purify the water using carbon filtration and chlorination. In 2009, they started operations with high hopes. They were thrilled because they had been able to meet the technical challenge of producing drinking water at very low costs.

But to their disappointment, few villagers stepped up to buy the clean water. Buy water? It just didn't make sense to these poor people, no matter how cheap it was. They did not believe the arsenic would affect them. Sadly, 95 percent of the plant remained unutilized.

The Veolia team brought in an anthropologist to help them understand what else was preventing the people from buying the water. One problem was that village women did not want to be seen by people outside their families. The culture of purdah was still sufficiently alive so that many women were not comfortable leaving their family compounds and walking to a central village outlet to get water. The Veolia team went back to the drawing board and came up with a solution: creating many outlets along the central pipeline so there was an outlet close to every family compound.

As the months passed, the team accepted the fact that to keep the operation going they needed to sell their water at higher prices to the few middle-class people who did have money and who understood the value of the purified water. By December of 2011, Grameen Veolia Water had still to break even, and the team had been told they must accomplish this within three years.

* * * * *

I was the only one in the restaurant of a downscale Miami hotel one morning in September 2010. Later that day I was scheduled for another in my series of interviews with Yunus. As I took the first bite of my scrambled eggs, Yunus strode into the restaurant, gave me a big smile, and sat down at the table next to mine. He explained that he was meeting some people for breakfast to talk about setting up social businesses in Haiti. They were already late.

Before I knew it, Yunus had turned the tables and was interviewing me. First he asked, "What topics are on the agenda for our interview?" and then he wanted to know more about my other writing. When I mentioned my book about Gypsies, he fired off a half dozen questions—wonderful, thought-provoking questions about these mysterious people. And he gave me his undivided attention as I responded to each one. I felt challenged and heard, personally met by him in some new way. He was off script and free of the usual lines that roll out so smoothly.

The conversation veered back to Yunus's concern that much of the enormous amount of money that was pouring into Haiti was being wasted because there was not enough infrastructure to handle it. His idea was to create a fund to support young people who wanted to start small businesses.

Chef José Andrés, who owns six high-end restaurants in Washington, D.C., and was one of those Yunus was supposed to be meeting for breakfast, had told Yunus, "I like your idea of social business." Yunus had responded,

"Why don't you train young Haitian boys and girls how to cook and sell delicious food, simple food that common people eat, so they can make a living for themselves?" Yunus's face glowed as he described to me how this would all unfold.

At this point, Andrés and two others arrived and my serendipitous time with Yunus came to an abrupt end. They had been looking for him all over the hotel.

Later that morning, when Yunus and I had our scheduled interview, there was an emotional tone that was qualitatively different from that in our earlier interviews. I think it was the unplanned meeting and our spontaneous conversation that made me finally different from the never-ending stream of people who interview Yunus but whom he doubts he will ever see again.

He went on to explain how in 2006 he had shifted his focus from microcredit to social business. He had come to realize that microcredit alone couldn't eliminate poverty. Social businesses, he now believed, not only had the potential to transform capitalism but also could become a significant way to improve the lives of the poor.

Yunus's full definition of a social business is a non-dividend, non-loss company that has as its purpose the solving of a social problem. He has written, "We have so many problems like the problem of unemployment, gender inequality, healthcare, maternal death, infant death, water and sanitation, environment, etc. In a social business the intention of the investor is to solve a problem, not to make any personal profit."[3] He describes a second kind of social business, which is profit-making. This business is dedicated to a social cause and is owned by poor people. The Grameen Bank is this second kind of social business.

According to Yunus, "The biggest flaw in our existing theory of capitalism lies in its misrepresentation of human nature. In the present interpretation of capitalism, human beings engaged in business are portrayed as one-dimensional beings whose only mission is to maximize profit. Once we recognize this flaw in our theoretical structure, the solution is obvious. We must replace the one-dimensional person in economic theory with a multidimensional person—a person who has both selfish and selfless interests at the same time. ... We see the need for two kinds of businesses: one for personal gain, another dedicated to helping others."[4] He is confident that there are many people who will find that the pleasure they get from solving problems and serving humanity is enough to keep them engaged.

Yunus presents his thoughts about and experiences with social business in his two recent books, *Creating a World Without Poverty: Social Business and the Future of Capitalism*, which appeared in 2007, and *Building Social Business: The New Kind of Capitalism That Serves Humanity's Most Pressing Needs*, which was published in 2010.

Yunus differentiates social businesses from the broader field of social entrepreneurship. According to him, a social business seeks to make a profit as well as to solve a social problem, while a social entrepreneur might work at a not-for-profit organization or a for-profit business. According to many social entrepreneurs, the key is simply that their organizations are trying to solve social problems. Yunus believes that grants from foundations and charitable donations sap the initiative of those who receive them and urges business to refuse such funds.

Despite his pronouncements and distinctions, Yunus is always considered a fellow social entrepreneur by everyone in the field—and he is fine with that. In books, articles, and films about social entrepreneurship, Yunus is hailed as a founding father; often his story is cited as the beginning.

Yunus has been promoting social business full time since 2006—talking about it, writing about it, and developing social businesses in Bangladesh and around the world. The Yunus Centre, which occupies the 15th floor of the Grameen Bank building in Dhaka, is the one-stop resource center for all of Yunus's social business activities. Lamiya Morshed is the director of the Centre as well as his PR person and scheduler. She has become the person who can speak and write for him. She decides who gets to see him for how long and which invitations he will accept. Anyone like me who wants to talk with Yunus soon recognizes the power she wields.

According to Yunus, Lamiya has the perfect kind of international background and exposure to run the Centre. Her father was an ambassador; she was born in Tokyo, spent time in Brazil as a child, and studied in France and Germany. Not only is she fluent in many languages but, more importantly, she has the personal and communication skills to speak with people from anywhere in a quiet, confident manner. Yunus told me, "She makes sure I get the messages coming from different countries and responds to them quickly because I can't go checking every single email. She prefers it if she does it; she understands what my response would be. She does a wonderful job, and particularly promoting social business."[5]

I was surprised by the Yunus Centre the first time I met with Lamiya, in 2010. I saw just one conference room and a large, almost empty, warehouse-like room where three or four young people were hard at work at their computers. I wondered how this handful of people could be managing the activities of a world leader like Yunus. But on second thought, the place seemed to reflect his values accurately—no frills, no unnecessary adornment, and a lean staff.

Yunus has established a number of other social businesses in Bangladesh focused on the healthcare issues of the rural poor. Grameen Kalyan (Healthcare), mentioned earlier, is one of them. It has set up 33 clinics, each affiliated with a Grameen Bank branch, and also sponsors several eye-care hospitals that perform low-cost cataract operations. In Bangladesh there is only one nurse for every three doctors. To address the lack of nurses in the country, Yunus has created a joint venture with Glasgow Caledonian University in Scotland to establish nursing colleges. The first class of students at the first of these colleges, Grameen Caledonian College of Nursing in Dhaka, arrived on March 1, 2010.

A number of other companies, including Pfizer, Johnson & Johnson, and GE Healthcare, are collaborating with Grameen on projects that are in development. A few years ago, Yunus asked executives of Adidas to develop a low-cost shoe that could protect the poor in Bangladesh from the parasites that are rampant in the countryside. By 2012, Adidas had figured out how to make a sneaker that could sell for less than $1.50 and was starting production in Bangladesh. He has also started a joint venture in Japan with a Japanese textile company to produce cheap sanitary napkins, which are not available in Bangladeshi villages.

Many of Yunus's social business projects are global. In 2011, Yunus was invited to China to launch a baby-food business that would operate as a social business. In addition, a delegation of Chinese leaders of for-profits and not-for-profits came to Bangladesh. They spent a whole day with Yunus, visiting a village and talking with him about microcredit and social business and how to replicate some of his ideas.

The Grameen Creative Lab, located in Germany, has become a second engine, along with the Yunus Centre, for promoting social business around the world. In 2008 Hans Reitz, who was interested in eliminating poverty, became intrigued by Yunus's approach. Yunus and Reitz see the world in much the same way and soon became friends. Today the Grameen Creative Lab has an international staff of young people trained in business who speak at events and consult to those interested in starting social businesses. In partnership with the Yunus Centre, they sponsor events like a World Wide Social Business Day and an annual Social Business Summit.

I had a chance to learn more about the Grameen Creative Lab when I talked with Saskia Bruysten, its co-CEO. Bruysten, a half-German and half-Canadian thirty-something, worked at the Boston Consulting Group earlier in her career. The first time she heard Yunus speak, she thought, "This man makes so much sense. Of course, in order to solve social problems, not-for-profits and NGOs need more business sense."[6] The second time she heard him speak, she went up to him and said she wanted to work with him. He steered her to Hans Reitz, with whom he was already working closely. Reitz hired her, and they have been working together ever since.

For several years, Bruysten has been creating a buzz about social business around the world. She often says in her presentations, "Money is boring—I am sticking with social business."[7] She communicates to her audiences of young people her passion for her work and the profound meaning that she derives from it.

Bruysten reports that the social businesses started by the Grameen Creative Lab are still in the very early stages of development. In Haiti they have hired a local team and created a fund that has made its first investment in a school to train entrepreneurs. In December 2011, the team was investigating about 25 other ideas for potential social businesses to fund. There are other teams working to start social businesses in Columbia, India, Brazil, Ghana, and Albania. After several years, the teams plan to turn over their projects to local teams and leave.

In 2011, Yunus and Bruysten formed a new and separate company called Yunus Social Business to focus solely on the implementation of social businesses. This leaves the hosting of events and promotion of social business to the Grameen Creative Lab. Bruysten is the CEO of the new venture, while Yunus owns 51 percent of the stock. She is thrilled with the chance to work closely with him.

Bruysten sees social business as a global movement, albeit a small movement. She does not expect that social businesses will be 50 percent of the world economy in

50 years, but thinks maybe they will make up 10 percent of it. She believes the concept is here to stay, especially since it has been endorsed by such institutions as the European Union. It can change the way social problems are solved, and it will pull businesses into addressing social problems. She cited the fact that Groupe Danone now has a sustainability board, as well as a regular board of directors, as one example of how this has worked.

Yunus sees universities and young people as critical to the spread of social business. Isabelle Heliot of Grameen Veolia Water says, "Yunus is young in his mind and he is at his very best when he is speaking to students."[8] Benoit Ringot, her colleague at Veolia, first heard Yunus speak in 2005 while a student at HEC, a prestigious business school in Paris. He remembers Yunus saying, "The economy is not stable and we have to imagine new ways dealing with social problems." Ringot continued, "Yunus was able to convince the hundred of us that heard him that day that the solutions he presented were good ones."[9] And hearing Yunus speak changed his life: five years later, he found himself arriving at a remote Bangladeshi village to develop Grameen Veolia Water Company.

Courses about social entrepreneurship are now being taught at hundreds of universities around the world, and some of them are focused specifically on social businesses. California State University Channel Islands

(CI), which opened in 2002, has established an Institute of Social Business that Yunus visited in 2010. Its website states, "Unencumbered by years of tradition, CI educates its students for the world they will inherit, with a focus that is international, multicultural, civically engaged, and interdisciplinary." At Glasgow Caledonian University in Scotland, there is both a Yunus Chair for Research in Social Business and Health, and a Yunus Centre for Social Business and Health. And in 2012 Yunus was named Chancellor of Glasgow Caledonian University.

In Japan, Kyushu University has created a Grameen Technology Lab. Both the University of Florence and the Asian Institute of Technology in Bangkok have established Yunus Centres, which focus on social business. And in France, HEC Paris, where Ringot studied, has created a social business chair, and the school offers a certificate in Social Business/Enterprise and Poverty.

As I learned more about Yunus's recent efforts to promote social business, I was struck by how often he has worked to promote the development of women and chosen them as colleagues. I still find this remarkable for a Muslim man in a Muslim country. Americans who have not witnessed firsthand the gender segregation in countries like Bangladesh may have a hard time understanding just how extraordinary this behavior has been. As managing director of the Grameen Bank, Yunus had promoted Nurjahan as his deputy. Nine of the 12 members of the Board of the Grameen Bank have always been village women who were borrowers from the Bank and therefore shareholders. As he turned his attention to social business, Yunus has trusted Lamiya with being his interface to the world. More recently, he has selected Saskia Bruysten as a partner for his new enterprise, Yunus Social Business.

For years, Yunus relentlessly promoted microcredit in rural Bangladesh. Now he is promoting social business with the same energy and drive, circling the globe over and over. Apparently he thrives on the constant work, though he dismissed my suggestion that maybe he is a workaholic. He did admit that there are some downsides to his way of working. He explained, "I am not the type of family person that I spend a lot of time with them. They've got used to it. It's not a good thing for them. They ask me, 'When are you visiting us next time?' although I live in Bangladesh. But I hardly live there. I am always someplace else."[10]

As for the future of social business, Yunus has said, "Gradually it will take shape and some of the seeds will sprout, some of them will not sprout, and people will see what resonates for them ... The whole thing is to make sense to an individual person. Whether they say, 'Ah, this is something I can do.'"[11] In *Building Social Business*, he wrote, "In just a few short years, social business has developed from a mere idea into a living, rapidly growing reality ... and [it] is now on the verge of exploding into one of the world's most important social and economic trends."[12]

Yunus remains optimistic about social business, even though the implementation of his projects in Bangladesh and elsewhere has been a bumpy road. Grameen Danone and Grameen Veolia Water, the flagship projects, have both faced ongoing challenges in reaching a point where they break even. The expansion of nursing colleges has also moved more slowly than anticipated. Although projects around the world are in their infancy, he sees that momentum is building.

If Yunus has not yet transformed capitalism, he is leading the way to an alternative kind of economy populated with hybrid organizations that combine the strengths of business and the mission-driven goals of not-for-profits. It is certainly not too soon to herald the success of Yunus in promoting the concept of social business. Since the financial meltdown of 2008, the numbers of those attracted to social business have grown exponentially.

In recent years, Yunus has continued to come up with new partnerships, new ventures, new ways of working, new ideas. Malcolm Gladwell, in his essay "Creation Myth," talks about certain entrepreneurs who are "wild geysers of creative energy."[13] That struck me as a wonderfully apt metaphor for Yunus. I have no doubts that since Yunus is presently directing his creative energy on social business, his results will be astounding, despite whatever else is happening in his life.

*Nurjahan as number two at the Bank in 2010 just
months before Yunus's ouster.*

Chapter Thirteen:
Ousted!

"The appeal is dismissed," proclaimed Chief Justice Haque to the crowd gathered in the courtroom of the Supreme Court in Bangladesh.[1] It was April 5, 2011, and Muhammad Yunus had lost the legal battle to hold on to his job as managing director of the Grameen Bank, a position he had held since 1983. He was not present, but he had told his staff that he would respect the ruling. How could this bizarre reversal of fortune happen to Yunus, the revered Nobel laureate? How could Yunus, the tireless champion of the poor, be treated this way?

More than a year before the ouster, I had turned to Mahfuz Anam, the editor of the English-language newspaper in Bangladesh, *The Daily Star*, to help me understand how Yunus was viewed in his own country. Mahfuz Anam's office was filled with piles of books, and the walls were papered with framed articles. A pleasant-looking man in his late 50s, Mahfuz Anam warned me that he was not unbiased about Yunus. He told me that every time he feels discouraged about his country and its situation, he goes to talk with Yunus and then feels better. We had been talking for less than five minutes when his phone rang. Prime Minister Sheikh Hasina wanted to see him immediately. A quick apology, and he was out the door.

When we reconvened several days later, Mahfuz Anam began with an analysis of how various factions of Bangladeshis feel about Yunus. "By far the greatest majority admire him immensely, for (a) what he has done for the poor, and (b) what honor he has brought to the country." He continued, "Here is Bangladesh. In some respects we are on the bottom. And in some other respects we are being emulated by the world... The credit is not solely to Yunus, but Yunus is the brightest of them all." [2]

He went on to explain that there are a number of groups that are critical of Yunus for wildly different reasons. Some people question whether his work has really helped the poor. Despite 30 years of microfinance, there are still millions of poor people, and the poor in the villages continue to get wiped out by floods or illness. Mahfuz Anam believes, however, that the largest group of critics thinks that the interest rates of the Grameen Bank are too high, higher than what commercial banks charge. These people just don't get that commercial banks collect collateral and don't send their staff out to the small villages the way Grameen does. That makes running Grameen expensive.

The religious base, who wields power in the villages, complains that Yunus is destroying the culture. They fear women will become loose characters or the divorce rate will go up. Then there are the intellectuals, the economists who think that although he received the Nobel Peace Prize and is now a world famous economist, they are the real economists.

According to Mahfuz Anam, a critical point in shaping how Yunus is viewed in Bangladesh was his brief and unsuccessful foray into national politics in 2007. The politics of Bangladesh had become polarized. There were two parties, two camps, two women prime ministers. "It was either Tweedledee or Tweedledum. One year we elected one of these two ladies. And the next year the other."[3]

In Bangladesh, in the 90 days before a national election, a caretaker government was often put in place. This government—which was allied with neither party— could, it was hoped, create a fair process. But in 2006, Mahfuz Anam continued, the caretaker government stayed in power much longer than usual. The interim government moved ahead with a very strong anti-corruption drive, and jailed many leaders, including the two women prime ministers for corruption.

At that point, Mahfuz Anam explained, people started thinking about third parties, and Yunus's name was naturally mentioned. "Who had the biggest name recognition? And, of course, he is a great communicator. And many people, including me, said to him, 'Why don't you join politics?' We also thought if there was a third party, then these two political parties would perhaps start behaving better."[4]

"However," he went on, "it's my impression he was not cut out for politics. He is a doer, not a talker. You have to do a lot of posturing, which doesn't suit his personality."[5]

"When Yunus announced his intentions in 2007, we saw clearly that people were not jumping on board. Given his prestige and his aura, people should have flocked behind him. And I think in normal circumstances they would have. So that was a big shock to him and also quite a realization for others who thought that people wanted an alternative... I think the timing was wrong. But at that time it looked as if he was taking advantage of the fact that the country was under emergency and that both these two leaders were in jail. In our culture, it is a big crime to have political ambition without being in politics. In addition, Yunus had not resigned from all his positions and it was not clear whether he would resign from them or not."

"Yunus's foray into politics happened in those circumstances, and the public misconceived it," Mahfuz Anam concluded. "But he quickly recovered from it and withdrew."[6]

Later, Yunus told me his side of this event. "Then this new caretaker government started taking all of these political leaders from both sides to jail. And with lots of corruption charges. So many people were coming and telling me, 'Why don't you form a political party?' When I said 'No,' people said, 'You don't want to disrupt your reputation, you don't care about the nation, it can go to hell.' So I started thinking maybe they have some truth in what they are saying. Maybe it's because of selfishness that I don't want to be involved. Because it's dirty. So I thought maybe let me try. So I went ahead."[7] In February 2007, Yunus wrote an open letter asking citizens for their views on his plan to float a new political party, Citizens' Power (Nagorik Shakti), dedicated to establishing proper leadership and good governance.

After he announced his intentions to start a new party, Yunus recalled, "Everybody is criticizing, everybody is shouting at me. So all kinds of reactions. People love you, people hate you. So I am standing alone, and in the meantime, all of the corrupt politicians were rallying around me. They think I will protect them from jail sentences. Then I went to the press and said 'I am not proceeding. I am not going to form a political party.'"[8]

When I asked Yunus if he thought it could have worked out differently or whether he made any miscalculations, he said, "I did the right thing. The fact for me was, they were not with me. I don't think about it. It's something that had to be done, I did it, and it didn't work out. I don't go back, I just keep moving. So you can't spend time regretting."[9]

Twenty-Seven Dollars and a Dream

In 2008, Sheikh Hasina, now out of jail, was elected prime minister by a landslide in an election in which over 80 percent of the electorate turned out. She knew, however, from her own experience just how quickly the tide can turn in politics and that she had to watch her back. When she was a young woman, her father and 18 other members of her family had been executed during a coup. She survived only because she happened to be out of the country at the time.

For years, Yunus had carefully fostered a positive relationship with Sheikh Hasina, going out of his way to include her in all his successes. He had created a significant role for her at the 1997 Microcredit Summit in Washington, D.C., she got the first phone call from GrameenPhone, and he invited her to be part of his entourage to Oslo when he received the Nobel Peace Prize.

But after 2008, it became clear that Sheikh Hasina did not forget about Yunus's bid for political power. She now saw him as an opponent, and she no longer championed microcredit. Her jealousy of his Nobel Prize was common knowledge. She had gone so far as to send emissaries to Nelson Mandela and others to make the case that she should receive the Nobel Peace Prize herself for her work with the hill tribes in Bangladesh. When Yunus received the Presidential Medal of Freedom from Obama in 2009, she never congratulated him.

I never met Sheikh Hasina when I was in Bangladesh but I did meet Khaleda Zia, her arch-rival. She and I sat together for a cup of tea. She seemed like a pleasant woman who spoke enough English so we could chat about our grandchildren for a few minutes. I didn't see her as a Margaret Thatcher, an iron-lady type of leader. But that was in the 1990s.

The next volley in the story of Yunus's ouster came in November 2010. A Danish documentary film, *Caught in Micro Debt*, which aired on Norwegian television, alleged serious misdoing on the part of Yunus and the Grameen Bank. It asserted that $100 million received from a Norwegian aid agency, NORAD, had been improperly transferred from the Grameen Bank to Grameen Healthcare, a not-for-profit sister organization. The film also claimed that the Grameen Bank charged exorbitant interest rates ranging from 30 to 200 percent.

Shortly afterward, the press reported that these allegations were false. Back in 1998, Norway had investigated the charges and concluded there was no improper use of funds and that the matter had been settled between NORAD and the Grameen Bank. But despite this, the incorrect allegations were repeated over and over in the press. Just a hint of wrongdoing on the part of Yunus, who often seemed too good to be true, made big news.

At this point, perhaps spurred on by the media frenzy, Prime Minister Sheikh Hasina jumped into the fray. She began a not-so-subtle campaign to disparage Yunus and force him from his position as managing director. She accused microcredit of "sucking blood from the poor," by charging excessively high interest rates.[10] Other officials in the government, including the foreign minister and the agriculture minister, as well as Sheikh Hasina's son and top officials in her political party, the Awami League, alleged more misdoing. They claimed Yunus had enriched himself at the expense of the poor, mismanaged the Bank, and engaged in fraud.

When all these stories hit the press in November 2010, Saskia Bruysten, of the Grameen Creative Lab in Germany, flew to Paris to join the people at Groupe Danone who set up a task force to support Yunus. Bruysten told me, "I knew he would never do anything that was not legal or take money."[11] The task force was certain that the accusations were false, and that it was some kind of a crazy attempt to take over the Grameen Bank. She reported that Yunus was absolutely shocked that people would make up such lies about him. He appeared calm, but after the bloodsucker comment he saw how serious the situation had become and acknowledged, "This is going downhill."

Bruysten remembers, "Those of us in Paris were worried because we knew what it meant to have the government against you in a non-democratic country. I don't think Yunus ever slept at all during this time." His inner circle, including Daley-Harris, Counts and their colleagues, Lamiya Morshed, Vidar Jorgensen, and the Danone people were in constant communication to discuss how to handle the crisis. Bruysten said, "Vidar, in particular, was on every important call and talked to every relevant person."[12] She explained that as the situation grew more dire, the task force worried about what would happen to the Bank, who might take over, and whether they would care about sustainability.

On March 2, 2011, the new chairman of the board of the Grameen Bank appointed by the government announced that Yunus had been dismissed from his position as managing director. The general manager of the Grameen Bank, a woman named Jannat-E-Quanine, responded with a statement for Yunus saying that he would be continuing in his office pending review of the legal issues surrounding the controversy.

Legally the government owns 25 percent of the Bank and had the right to appoint three of the 12 board members, including its chairperson. But Yunus and his staff claimed that the government had little reason to intervene in operations of the Bank and that hiring and firing of the managing director was up to the entire board. Yunus and the nine independent directors (women from the villages) petitioned the High Court to invalidate his dismissal.

A spokesman for the central bank of Bangladesh said Yunus had been in his position illegally, since he had not sought its approval when he was reappointed to the post of managing director in 2000. The finance minister, A.M.A. Muhith, claimed that the 71-year-old Yunus was violating the mandatory retirement laws for commercial banks, which require executives to retire at 60 years. This is the same man who had helped Yunus get legal status for his bank way back in 1983. He was the one who had increased the government's share of ownership of the Grameen Bank from 40 to 60 percent at the last minute.

Muhith reported he had been trying to convince Yunus for a year that it was time for him to retire. "We are proud of him, but it is also true that an illegal matter cannot go on for an indefinite time."[13] His argument was a bit ironic, since Muhith himself was 77.

The U.S. ambassador to Bangladesh met with Muhith on March 3. He told reporters that the United States was "deeply troubled by the process here that is trying to remove Professor Yunus."[14] Hundreds of people from around the world sent messages of support. Hillary Clinton and John Kerry sent statements. Twenty-seven members of Congress sent a letter to Prime Minister Sheikh Hasina expressing their concern about the government's actions.

In Bangladesh, on March 5, thousands of borrowers, students, and supporters protested what was happening.

They formed human chains in several cities to demonstrate their support for Yunus. In addition, 3.7 million borrowers signed a petition requesting that Yunus stay at the Bank.

A member of Yunus's legal team said on March 7, "All these years [the government] never questioned Yunus's reappointment. This raises suspicions they are part of a character assassination."[15] The legal expert asserted that, because the Grameen Bank is not a regular bank and was created under a separate statute, the central bank of Bangladesh does not have the right to remove officials of the Grameen Bank.

Yunus said, "I am riding the tiger. I cannot just get off the tiger without drawing the attention of that tiger. So I have to very quietly do it."[16] On March 8 Yunus appealed to the Supreme Court.

On March 21, David Bornstein wrote in the *New York Times*, "It has taken 35 years of painstaking effort to build Grameen into a world-class institution that serves millions of poor people… Anyone who cares about international development, microfinance, or social entrepreneurship should pay attention. It is not just the largest microlender in the world… It is also a leading example and inspiration for millions of citizen-led organizations that have been established in recent decades to address social problems that governments have failed to solve."[17]

As the controversy continued, the pressure on the Bangladeshi government mounted. On March 24, Robert Blake, U.S. Assistant Secretary of State, accompanied by James Wolfensohn, the former president of the World Bank, met with Sheikh Hasina, Muhith, and Yunus in Dhaka. Blake told a news conference that if there wasn't a compromise, it would have an effect on bilateral relations. He did not explain what that meant, but he urged that they come up with a compromise solution.

The Awami League general secretary, Mahbub-Alam Hanif, announced that he did not want any foreign interference into the country's internal matters. At another time he claimed that thousands of people had become beggars due to Yunus.

On April 27, a Bangladeshi government panel claimed that the nine women on the board of directors of Grameen were ill-equipped to fulfill their oversight role because they weren't educated and most of them were illiterate. The panel called for the Grameen Bank to be restructured because of its poor governance and because it was circumventing the law.

The government of Bangladesh set up a review committee to investigate all the allegations against the Grameen Bank. The Bank fully cooperated with this committee. Its report, which was released some months later, cleared Yunus and the Grameen Bank of all wrongdoing, mismanagement, and personal corruption.

They found that the matter of the NORAD funds had been settled amicably between the agency and the Bank back in 1998. They also discovered that the Grameen Bank had the lowest interest rates of any microfinance institution in Bangladesh, with 20 percent being its top rate. Supporters of Yunus and the Bank tried to get out the word about these findings. But, as is typical, once serious allegations have been made, a black cloud of uncertainty hovered around Yunus.

On May 12, 2011, Yunus resigned from his position as managing director. It was a month after his appeal had been rejected by the Supreme Court. In his comments, he emphasized the importance of maintaining the independence of the Bank. He and his supporters worried that if there were a government takeover of the Bank, there would be dire consequences. Those with savings at the Bank might rush to withdraw their money. The lending process might come to a full stop. The government might take over some of the social businesses that Yunus had founded.

But by April 2012 this had not happened. The Bank was conducting business and an interim managing director was in place. Yunus was tending to his social business ventures, creating new partnerships and new ventures every month, and promoting the concept of social business.

Bruysten told me in late 2011, "In my eyes, he has not changed at all... He works like crazy, never taking a single day off. Now he is tired after months of explaining things over and over, having to fight back. He is completely tired, and I could imagine he has become disillusioned about the press and the government. He has aged a lot."[18]

When I spoke with Vidar Jorgensen in 2012, he said the charges were laughable. He added that he has never seen Yunus down or discouraged. Yunus is as active as ever, but he is now somewhat limited in what he can accomplish. Jorgensen feels Yunus has lost perhaps 5 to 10 percent of his effectiveness because the government is making life difficult. The Otto Group, a multinational company, for example, was not given a license by the government to start up a social business in Bangladesh, even though they were prepared to allocate $31 million to get their venture up and running.

The question remains: how to make sense of what happened? Clearly there was a political vendetta on the part of Sheikh Hasina. But it cannot be that simple. There were other people who joined her.

The next question to ask is: What was Yunus's responsibility for creating an environment where this ouster could happen? There is of course his misstep in politics, which seems with hindsight to be crucial in the unraveling of his relationship with Sheikh Hasina. But this was not followed by any indications or actions on his part that suggested he was the slightest bit interested in political power.

Yunus does have a history of some failed relationships—Dipal Barua, his former number two, and Iqbal Quadir come to mind. Muzammel Huq and A.M.A Muhith are two other allies who turned against him. Perhaps he could have paid more attention to mending fences.

In 2011, Muzammel Huq, the new chairman of Grameen, commented to the press, "I think he is a good man with a small heart. He cannot give credit to anyone but himself."[19] From the reports, Huq smiled as he said this, so the pun was probably intended.

Michaela Walsh, founder of Women's World Banking, had a similar view. She said to me in 2010, "Yunus had a golden voice and he charmed people. You can't take away what he has done. You couldn't not like Yunus, but he wasn't loved." She recalled how once at a meeting someone interrupted Yunus and said, 'You sound like the Messiah. But you never give anyone else any credit.'"[20]

Many people I interviewed before the ouster—academics, Yunus's family members, experts in development—told me that for years the press and others have been hungry to hear anything negative about him. Many people felt he got too many prizes, too much attention, too much adoration. Another positive story about Yunus was not news. A flaw or wrongdoing—now that was news. This partly explains how the accusations against Yunus got such traction.

So maybe Yunus held on to his managing director position too long and should have announced a date for his retirement from the Bank. And maybe it's true that he could have given more credit to others. I believe he was caught in a power dynamic where a jealous, vindictive, and ruthless prime minister was determined to take him down and to use all the power she had to accomplish it. And sadly, there are always some people who will side with the head of state no matter how unjustified his or her position may be. From all the evidence I have seen, the ouster of Yunus from his position at the Grameen Bank was unjust and undeserved. It was especially ungrateful of his own Prime Minister to remove him from his position after he has spent his entire lifetime working to end poverty and after he has brought so much honor to Bangladesh.

The Grameen Bank Headquarters.

Chapter Fourteen:

Microcredit Under Attack

I had come to Spain in November, 2011, to attend the Global Microcredit Summit, wanting to see for myself how Yunus was doing six months after his ouster and resignation in May from the Grameen Bank. I was aware that microfinance had also taken a pummeling in recent months. To add to the industry's other troubles, researchers who had conducted randomized studies had published new findings indicating that microcredit made little impact on poverty. A few observers of the scene had even predicted the demise of the industry. I wanted to talk with participants at the Summit who came from many countries to get their sense of what was happening.

As I entered the main hall of the conference center in Valladolid, a city an hour north of Madrid, I surveyed the milling crowd hoping to catch a glimpse of Yunus. Sure enough, I soon spotted him striding down the corridor surrounded by a small covey of young people. He saw me, grabbed my hand, and pulled me along beside him as he made his way to his next meeting. He has this way of sweeping up people wherever he goes.

Several hours later I saw Yunus again. He was flashing a smile, surrounded this time by a large crowd of mostly

young men—Asians and Europeans in blue jeans and
a few Africans in long, flowing, native garb. He was
patiently posing with two or three people at a time so
each of them could be in a small group picture with him.
He was obviously enjoying himself and was clearly still
their rock star.

The Global Microcredit Summit in Spain was taking
place just about a year after the airing of the Danish
documentary film that had set off a chain reaction
of allegations of misdoing by Yunus and microcredit
organizations. These attacks shocked the world, in
part because both Yunus and the industry had been
the darlings of so many for so long. Microcredit had
united those in non-profits who were dedicated to
ending poverty, those in the development field who
wanted to help poor people achieve self-sufficiency, and
entrepreneurs who saw microfinance as a way to make
money while doing good. FINCA, ProMujer, Accion,
SEWA, Kiva, and dozens of other organizations had
attracted millions of dollars from people and foundations
that wanted to help the downtrodden.

In 2011, thousands of microfinance institutions were
scattered around the planet. While many had gotten their
original inspiration from Yunus and the Grameen Bank
model, most of these organizations had developed their
own ways of working, which diverged in varying degrees
from the Grameen model. Almost all of them differed in

one crucial dimension from Grameen—they did not have the legal status of a bank. This was important, because it meant they could not accept deposits. Without the flow of funds that come with savings accounts, it has been difficult for some microfinance institutions to reach the breakeven point and to become profitable. Grameen, on the other hand, had focused on savings for a decade and in recent years had made a profit. It had been able to distribute a small dividend to its shareholders—that is, its borrowers, all of whom owned at least one share.

Yunus has often proclaimed that microcredit will lift poor people out of poverty. In almost every speech he says that he looks forward to the time when people will have to go to a museum to see what poverty looks like. To measure progress towards his goal, Yunus developed 10 indicators that signaled when a family in rural Bangladesh had crossed the line out of poverty.

1. The family lives in a house worth at least $370 and all family members sleep on cots or beds.

2. The family's drinking water is pure.

3. All children over six attend or have attended primary school.

4. The member's weekly repayment sum is at least $3.

5. The family uses a hygienic latrine.

6. All the family has sufficient clothes, blankets, and mosquito netting.

7. The family has a garden or fruit trees to fall back on.

8. The member has an average balance of $75 in her savings account.

9. The member has the ability to feed her family three meals a day throughout the year.

10. The family members can pay for medical expenses in the event of illness.[1]

From 1997 on, Yunus and the Bank collected data to determine exactly how many people had escaped from poverty based on these indicators. Their data indicated that 5 percent of their borrowers moved out of poverty each year.

Yunus was not the only one interested in assessing the impact of microcredit and the Grameen Bank on poverty. Beginning in the 1980s, researchers from around the world had arrived on his doorstep wanting to conduct their own assessments of the Grameen Bank. In a 2010 interview, Yunus told me that these evaluators would arrive as skeptics, but after spending some months conducting their own research and visiting branches of the Bank, would end up positive about what was going on at Grameen.

Of course, there had always been critics. In 1998, Jonathan Morduch of the Economics Department of Harvard University and the Hoover Institute of Stanford University presented a paper entitled "Does Microfinance

Really Help the Poor?"[2] The paper was widely circulated
and persuasively cast doubts about the impact of
microcredit. In 2001, one of Daniel Pearl's last articles
to appear in the *Wall Street Journal* suggested that the
Grameen Bank was in serious trouble, and it too made a
big splash.[3] But these critical voices were unusual, and,
in general, Yunus and microfinance were favorites of the
media.

Then in 2006 reports from India about microcredit
gone haywire caught the world's attention. It was
reported that 200 people in the state of Andhra Pradesh
on the southeast coast of India had committed suicide
because of their accumulated indebtedness from small
loans. Articles about debt collectors' bullying of their
poor clients and exorbitant interest rates went viral.

Some months later, the Reserve Bank of India
dismissed the allegations of harassment and suicides as
isolated incidents. But the attacks in India had tarnished
the image of microfinance everywhere. An article
appeared in the *Economic Times* calling 2006 "the year
of microfinance bashing."[4]

Despite these events, the microfinance industry
continued to grow fast, especially in India. Vikram
Akula, who had been a protégé of Yunus's, headed SKS
Microfinance, known as the Starbucks of microfinance
because it had expanded so rapidly. Akula was one of
those people whose life had been changed forever when

he read Yunus's book *Banker to the Poor.* He was a student in Chicago at the time, and he soon set off for Bangladesh to learn about microfinance from the master.

Yunus knew Akula well and liked him, "So we lent him money to start." And that is how SKS began. The company prospered and received a number of awards, including an Excellence Award from the Grameen Foundation. The future looked rosy for Akula and for SKS.

But, as Yunus related to me, Akula gradually shifted his focus away from helping the poor toward making money. Yunus was upset by the high interest rates that SKS was charging. He recalled, "I kept saying, 'This is not right.' But Akula said, 'No, I am very committed to the ideals and so on.' I told him, 'You are facilitating more poor people getting exploited that way. So the more money you make, the more exploitation. Loan sharks are doing the same thing.'"

After a long pause, Yunus added, "So I wouldn't say he's deliberately doing it as a corrupt person. He thinks this is the right thing."[5]

In 2010, SKS held an initial public offering (IPO) to raise more capital. The IPO raised nearly $350 million and Akula, chairman of SKS Microfinance, privately sold shares that put $13 million into his own pocket. Yunus said, "This is an idea that is repulsive to me."[6]

Around the world, those in the microfinance industry were sharply divided. Some, like Yunus, believed it was just plain wrong to make huge profits off the backs of the poor and to charge interest rates of 90 percent or more. Others, like Akula, believed that microcredit organizations needed to attract capital from private equity investors and to charge very high interest rates. They explained that the administrative costs of small loans and outposts in the villages made this necessary. It was just business sense to do what you needed to do to make a profit.

In 2010, once again, there were reports of poor people in Andhra Pradesh who had become so overwhelmed by debt from their small loans that they committed suicide. And there were new articles about the exorbitant interest rates that some microfinance institutions charged their clients. The state government of Andhra Pradesh passed harsh regulations that brought microfinance there to a halt. Many borrowers in Andhra Pradesh stopped repayments on their loans. In addition, commercial banks stopped lending to microfinance institutions in all regions of India, not just Andhra Pradesh. In November, the *New York Times* ran a cover story, "Microcredit in India Is Imperiled by Defaults."[7] The microfinance industry in India, which had been growing at the astonishing rate of 90 percent between 2002 and 2009, slowed to a mere 7 percent in 2010.

SKS reported a loss in May, 2011. The price of its shares dropped 70 percent as a result of borrowers' stopping payment on their loans in Andhra Pradesh.

Akula remained hopeful, saying "I still think it's a solid business." He did admit, "SKS reacted too slowly to the criticism of its business by politicians and community leaders."[8]

I had looked forward to meeting Akula at the Summit in Spain, where he had been scheduled to give a workshop on IPOs. Instead, word came that he had resigned as chairman of SKS.

Sanjay Sinha, managing director of Micro Credit Rating International (M-CRIL), put the situation in some perspective.[9] He said that the microfinance industry, which had been a nimble hare for the past 20 years, had become a raging bull. He blamed the industry's troubles in India on their relentless drive for growth at all costs. He believed relationships between lenders and borrowers, which in the past had usually been close, had soured. Stories circulated about borrowers who had taken out four or five loans from different microfinance organizations and were running from meeting to meeting to make repayments, using one loan to pay back another.

But, Sinha asserts, it was the state regulations in Andhra Pradesh that felled the raging bull. Sinha believes that the major motivation of government officials in India in placing crippling restrictions on microfinance institutions was their desire to protect and support their own government programs that were in competition with the other microfinance programs. The tension in India between the government and these private institutions had existed for years. But it had increased dramatically in the last few years, and the government's hostility was much more apparent.

While microfinance continued to expand rapidly in Mexico, South America, Africa, and much of Asia, a survey in 2011 found people in many countries concerned about the directions that microfinance was taking in their countries. Issues identified were the growing commercialism, increased focus on growth at all costs, the demand for profitability, and mission drift. Pakistan, Bosnia, Nicaragua, and Morocco all experienced crises in their microfinance industry similar to that in India, and other countries looked ripe for a crisis.

In addition to all these difficulties, there was a second kind of assault on microfinance that came from academic researchers who studied the impact of microcredit on poverty. In 2005, Counts asked Nathanael Goldberg, an expert in the field of international development who had been chief of staff for the Microcredit Summit Campaign, to take stock of what was known about the impact of microcredit. Goldberg found much evidence that microfinance was working. "And so on the one hand we could feel really good about that. But it all seemed kind of murky. People who wanted to be sure that their investment in microfinance was going to create a positive impact didn't necessarily have enough to go on."[10] Others began to speak vehemently about the need for new studies where participants were chosen randomly and where there were control groups. By 2010, a number of researchers had conducted studies with randomized selection of subjects.

The preliminary findings of these so-called "randomistas" sent a shock wave through academia and the microfinance industry. Dean Karlan, an economics professor at Yale and author of one of these new studies, put it this way, "Microcredit is not a transformational panacea that is going to lift people out of poverty. There might be little pockets of people here and there of people who are made better off, but the average effect is weak if not nonexistent."[11] He told me that his results were important because in the past the ideology around microcredit and small loans had prevented money from going in other directions, such as savings or insurance programs, that could have done more for poor people. Other new studies suggested there was more impact on poverty from loans to "better off" poor people than to the poorest of the poor.

Abhijit Baneerjee and Esther Duflo, economists at MIT's Jameel Poverty Action Lab, found slightly more positive impact from small loans than Karlan had. When Duflo was asked why microcredit didn't boost health and education outcomes, she wondered why anyone had expected all those things to happen. About microcredit she said, "It's useful, but it's not like the miracle drug to end poverty."[12] Of course, one of the reasons there were such high expectations for the impact of small loans was that Yunus had so skillfully proposed exactly that. For decades, he had repeated his core message that microcredit could eliminate poverty in the foreseeable future.

Proponents of microcredit rose up to defend it from the attacks of the "randomistas."They argued that the time-frame of this new research—many studies were as short as 18 months—meant that their findings could not possibly be the whole story. They pointed to the phenomenal growth of microcredit around the world as proof that it must be of value to borrowers. But Florent Bedecarrats, a French research fellow at the Sorbonne, pointed out that of the 154 studies of microfinance since 1980, a good number had found microcredit as having a neutral or negative impact on poverty. He also suggested that because there has been so much focus on proving whether or not microcredit has an impact on poverty there has been little support for alternative approaches and for more qualitative research.

David Roodman's widely acclaimed book, *Due Diligence:An Impertinent Inquiry into Microfinance*, which appeared in 2012, is an evenhanded analysis of the existing research. Roodman, a senior fellow at the Center for Global Development in Washington, wrote his book in an open process, sharing chapters on his blog and incorporating feedback he received as he went along. I told him, by the way, that I didn't find his book all that impertinent. Maybe if you have the name Roodman you feel the least you can be is a bit impertinent.

When we talked about Yunus, Roodman told me he sees the world as having playwrights and critics. Yunus is clearly a playwright—a visionary, creative person—while Roodman sees himself as a critic. He said, "I am concerned about evidence and rigor. I see Yunus's weaknesses as oversimplification and rigidity." Then, moving to balance things a bit, he added, "I believe he is seen as more simplistic than he actually is." He explained that Yunus has not paid enough attention to the differing conditions that microfinance institutions face around the world and how much harder it has been for them to be profitable than it was for him. Grameen's legal status as a bank, in particular, was a key factor in its success. Roodman concluded, "Credit is a dangerous thing—you can get people in trouble with it, and there is a complexity that Yunus doesn't acknowledge."[13]

* * * * *

Queen Sofia of Spain slipped into a seat two rows ahead of me. I was waiting for Workshop #37, billed as a "Conversation with Industry Pioneers," to begin. Queen Sofia looked like a suburban grandmother with her nicely coiffed brown hair and expensive suit. Her entrance went unnoticed. On the other hand, when Yunus walked into the room a few moments later, all heads turned. Many in the audience stood up to get a better look and phones shot into the air. The woman from the Philippines sitting next to me whispered with reverence, "He is our leader."

As the session began, the conversation among the panelists was easy and warm. The pioneers were obviously fond of each other and having a good time. At one point a younger woman who had just assumed a leadership role in a microfinance institution was invited to join them at the table at the front of the room. A few minutes later, she asked Yunus about succession at the Grameen Bank. I sat up—she was daring to talk about the elephant in the room, Yunus's recent ouster from Grameen. He answered in a curiously monotone voice, "There is a proper process in place for selecting a managing director." She asked again, and then again, in slightly different ways, how Yunus felt about current happenings at the Grameen Bank. I waited anxiously to see how Yunus would handle her grilling. The audience was hushed and tense. He looked serious but not angry, and he repeated without emotion, "There is a good process in place." She had hit a brick wall. She could not get him to open up or to share his feelings. Minutes later, as the "old boys" picked up the conversation, the mood turned jovial once more. I realized I had just witnessed

Yunus under attack. He was stoic and polite, but he would not show anger in public and he would not fight.

Later I met Nurjahan in the hallway and she told me there had been some disturbing news from the Bank that day. The process for selecting a new managing director was not going well.

Despite all the various kinds of attacks that microcredit has received in recent years, the buzz at the conference was positive. Workshop presenters reported their statistics with pride, explained how they were expanding services, and announced new projects that were in process, such as a Seal of Excellence. Though it was often acknowledged that microfinance needed to adapt to changing times, for the participants at the Summit, it was business as usual. There were, however, a number of people who were asking hard questions about the health of the microfinance movement.

And there have been changes. Sam Daley-Harris, the major organizer of all the Microcredit Summits for the last 15 years, announced that he was leaving the Microcredit Summit Campaign and introduced his successor at the Summit. And Yunus was no longer at the Grameen Bank. I sensed that it was the end of an era for microfinance as well as for Yunus.

Obama presents the Medal of Freedom, America's highest civilian award, to Yunus in 2009.

Chapter Fifteen:

He Changed the World

Nurjahan's email to me had an ominous tone. "There are some things that cannot be shared over mail. Professor Yunus has been very busy, as usual. I could tell you more about him had we met face to face." A few weeks earlier in March, 2012, I had called Nurjahan to find out how Yunus was doing. She cut the interview short and requested that I send her all my questions about Yunus by email. Now it seemed she was putting me off for a second time. Questions ricocheted inside my head. How was Yunus really doing, and what was happening in Bangladesh?

I called Jahangir, one of Yunus's younger brothers, for more information. He is the brother who hosts a television show about current events in Bangladesh. He sounded a bit depressed as he told me, "I was shocked by the ruling party's harsh criticisms of Yunus. People in Bangladesh feel like they must support Sheikh Hasina and the government. While a few people continue to publically express support for Yunus, I was told it was better for me not to defend him." He added softly, "I became silent on these issues."

Jahangir went on to say, "Supporters of Yunus have been concerned for months that the government would go after his other companies, but so far the government has been slow to take further actions against him. The government faces elections in September, 2013, which will be a huge challenge. With the elections grabbing their attention, I hope that issues concerning Yunus may no longer be a priority for them."[1]

Next, I talked with Barbara Parfitt, the principal of the new Grameen Caledonian College of Nursing located in Dhaka.[2] She reported that since Yunus left his position at the Bank in 2011, progress on the new campus for the college outside the city has been slowed. "While before, just the word Grameen opened doors, now approvals from the government don't come at all or come months after we request them. We just smile when they refuse to help us and say, 'Thank you.'"

When I asked Lamiya Morshed, director of the Yunus Centre, how she thought things were going, she put a more positive face on the current situation. "Yunus's reputation has not been tarnished, and everyone in Bangladesh knows that the whole thing is just politics. Nobody buys it." She added, "If anything, his stature is enhanced; he is getting more attention on social business, and he is still receiving new awards for his work."[3]

When I asked Yunus in April how he was doing, he told me that the process to select his permanent replacement at the Bank has stalled. "The government will not approve the Selection Committee that the Board has put forth because I am on the Committee and the head of it." But he quickly turned the conversation to an upcoming trip to Atlanta and other current projects. He was upbeat.[4]

* * * * *

As I began to pull together my thoughts about Yunus's impact on the world, of course I wondered whether this most recent chapter of his life with its tensions and difficulties would affect how he would be seen in history. Whatever the ultimate answer, to clarify my own thinking I needed to consider his accomplishments against the backdrop of progress in Bangladesh since 1971.

Bangladesh is now the seventh most populated country in the world, with 164 million people. Life expectancy has risen for everyone; for women it has been breathtaking, rising from 57 years to 70. Fertility rates have dropped—from an average of 6 pregnancies per woman to 2.6 per woman. More than 87 percent of children are now enrolled in primary school, and Bangladesh has achieved gender parity in primary and secondary education.

The poverty rate in Bangladesh has declined from over 60 percent to 40 percent. Income per capita has risen from $664 to $1,700 per year, figured at today's rates. The garment industry has been growing fast, and

Bangladesh is now the second largest apparel-exporting nation. The minimum wage has been raised to about $36 a month. The UN has recognized Bangladesh as one of a small group of countries that is well on its way to achieving some of its Millennium Development Goals by 2015. They cite significant progress in Bangladesh in the areas of eradicating extreme poverty, reducing child mortality, access to safe water, and education.

At the same time, many pockets of extreme poverty remain. Drop-out rates in primary education are extremely high. Healthcare in the countryside is grossly inadequate. Women still live without the freedom to come and go that Western women take for granted. Climate change and rising sea levels pose a real threat since most of the country is only a few feet above sea level. Corruption remains a problem.

* * * * *

In my view, Yunus's role as champion of microcredit has been the crowning achievement of his life. Microcredit has literally opened the doors of legitimate financial services to millions of poor people. Yunus was the one who proved to the world that it was practical to lend to the poor without demanding collateral. His voice sparked the spread of microcredit around the world and led to more opportunities for those at the bottom of the economic pyramid everywhere.

"Microfinance remains one of a handful of key interventions that play a major role in advancing people out of poverty," according to Michael Chu, senior lecturer at the Harvard Business School and an expert in microfinance and social enterprise.[5] Today, however, no one sees microcredit as the single mechanism that will eliminate poverty in the near future. Years ago, microcredit evolved into the larger concept of microfinance, and now poverty experts look to other financial services such as savings, pension plans, and insurance as major tools in the war on poverty. In addition, development experts agree that addressing the needs of the poor in the areas of healthcare, education, housing, and energy is also critical.

The establishment of the Grameen Bank and the model of banking that Yunus developed there was another major achievement. He grew the Bank from a single outpost in one small village to a huge bank serving more than eight million poor people in Bangladesh. The Grameen model that was adopted around the world eliminates collateral, focuses on women as borrowers, and forms borrowers into small groups that meet weekly.

Over many years, Yunus improved the Bank's finance, hiring, training, oversight, evaluation, and communication systems—discovering by trial and error how to make them more effective. He decentralized the Grameen Bank and organized its structure so he could hold each part accountable as it grew. His ability to grow his Bank for the poor, to take it to scale, and to have it become sustainable was ground-breaking. Few of those who have tried to replicate his model in other lands have come anywhere close to his level of success.

Yunus's focus on lending to women was also pioneering. Small loans led to the empowerment of millions of women not only in Bangladesh but in all countries where microfinance institutions have been established. In Bangladesh, before the Grameen Bank, 98 percent of those who used banking services were men; by 2006, at the Grameen Bank, this was reversed, as 97 percent of its borrowers were women. Obtaining credit helped a woman economically by enabling her to start or develop a small business, buy a house or some land, or grow her husband's business. Grameen housing loans, which stipulated that a house must be in a woman's name only, had a big impact. The dynamics of many families shifted rapidly.

Yunus's approach to banking brought about an interesting mix of revolutionary change in women's social patterns and conservation of much of the traditional culture. Women who had been isolated in their compounds attended weekly meetings beyond them. They made new acquaintances and friends outside their families. The Sixteen Decisions that were part of the Grameen way pointed women toward better health and increased self-esteem. Women still remained in their homes, however, taking care of their children as they worked, and in many ways their lives were unchanged.

Today, when the Muslim world is confronted with the need to modernize and the pathway is not clear, Yunus provides a powerful role model for constructive leadership. He shows how to integrate Western and Eastern ideas and how to bring about change without destroying the social fabric.

Since 2006, Yunus has turned his prodigious energies to promoting social business, and he has achieved impressive results. He has been speaking about social business almost non-stop at universities and organizations around the world, and he has established pilot projects like Grameen Danone and Grameen Veolia in Bangladesh as well as in a variety of countries including Haiti, Bosnia, Columbia, Japan, and China. Many of these projects have had difficulties becoming profitable or breaking even. For now, it is too soon to judge the significance of the role that social businesses will eventually play in the world economy, or to estimate how much headway they will make in addressing the social problems they set out to confront.

There is, for sure, growing excitement about the concept. Yunus once again is striking a chord that resonates with people around the world. I met with one recent recruit, Leonard Lerer of the Innovative Finance

Foundation in Baden, Switzerland. He told me how, after hearing Yunus speak for the first time, he decided to go to Bangladesh to see for himself what was happening. "I was an instant convert," he said with a grin. Now he is bringing the resources of his foundation to fund healthcare projects in Bangladesh.

As I ponder all of Yunus's achievements, I also want to acknowledge his mistakes and give them the weight they are due. I consider that his failure to develop a succession plan was a major error in judgment. He should have had a successor groomed and ready to take over any time, and as he entered his sixties it would have been wise to make public the date by which he would leave the Bank. Yunus also failed to hire enough young, newly trained, and technology-savvy managers to keep Grameen on the cutting edge. He clung too long to his old pals for top leadership positions.

Yunus has often criticized microfinance institutions that charge interest rates higher than those of the Grameen Bank. I believe he could have expressed more appreciation of the fact that conditions in other countries make it hard, maybe impossible, to offer interest rates as low as Grameen's, since few of them have the legal status and privileges of a bank.

According to Michael Chu, "Yunus missed a grand opportunity to be the spokesman for the entire microfinance industry. Instead, Yunus saw himself as speaking for the Grameen Bank and as an advocate for the Grameen model. In recent years he increasingly aligned himself against the more commercial models of microfinance, which make up the majority of microfinance institutions. So this has limited the leadership role he plays today."[6]

Perhaps Yunus's most damaging misstep was his brief foray into politics in 2007. Although he had frequently expressed mistrust of governments, for decades he had demonstrated political savvy in working with the government of Bangladesh to achieve favorable conditions for the Grameen Bank. But this came to a sudden halt after his failed bid for leadership. Since that time, Sheikh Hasina has seen Yunus as an opponent, if not an enemy, and his attempts at relationship-building have yielded no change in her attitude. Now he is discovering just how difficult it is for any institution to operate successfully without the goodwill of its government.

Yunus seems to have the ability to tune out his failures and losses. Even after his dismissal from the Grameen Bank, he has been working at his usual pace. He has always kept moving ahead when important relationships have soured. It seems that Yunus is not self-reflective or interested in his interior life; he is above all a man of action. I believe his abiding confidence in the importance of his work enables him to stay the course no matter what happens.

His successes have come at a cost. His life has been all about work. He does not have hobbies or other interests. He does not take vacations or go to social events. It is a Spartan lifestyle that few would choose. He gave up his first marriage for his work. He did not see his daughter Monica for a number of years when she was growing up. His family has always taken a back seat. He stays in touch with his sister and brothers by phone. While he is easy to like and he connects with all sorts of people with ease, he does not seem to have close, intimate relationships. For all the warmth and friendliness, he seems to have an invisible wall around him that holds people at bay.

* * * * *

Whatever mistakes he may have made, and whatever the personal costs, it is clear that Muhammad Yunus changed the world. Understanding *how* he was able achieve such dazzling results provides important information for all those interested in making a difference in the world or in their organizations. His ability to be so successful begins with the many gifts he was born with—gifts of brilliance, creativity, energy, an optimistic temperament, and charisma. Those who want to be change agents would do well to have such an endowment.

But it is seven patterns of action that are most important in explaining Yunus's phenomenal success.

Together they provide lessons for all change-makers and a roadmap for those who seek to make a real difference in their organizations or in the world. (See page 267.)

The first of Yunus's patterns of action is setting forth a vision and sticking with it. Day after day, decade after decade, he has stayed the course, struggling against all kinds of obstacles to bring his dream of a world without poverty into reality. His vision has been compelling enough to continue to motivate his employees and broad enough to inspire millions of others. It is his singleness of purpose that has been so important.

The second pattern of action is how Yunus has communicated relentlessly. He has communicated across, down, and beyond the organization, and his communication has always been two-way. He carefully read the lengthy weekly reports required of his managers, and for years he visited every branch of the Bank, hearing first-hand about the concerns of staff and borrowers. He has communicated to the world at large through a barrage of newsletters, reports, articles, books, and speeches.

Yunus's third pattern of action is building a team that owned his dream. He chose his leaders from his colleagues and students at Chittagong University who shared his vision. The thousands of Grameen employees have formed a larger team. After their long and rigorous training period, employees who were not committed to helping the poor left for greener pastures and higher salaries. And then there were the others like Alex Counts at the Grameen Foundation, Sam Daley-Harris of the Microcredit Campaign, and Vidar Jorgensen who, while not employees, were part of an informal team of people dedicated to realizing his vision.

Being flexible is a fourth pattern of action that has been key to Yunus's success. While his vision of ending poverty has remained the same, he has been ready to change his goals, strategy, tactics, and focus as circumstances evolve. He has taken his cues from what worked, not from preconceived theoretical abstractions. Two examples: the way he transformed his basic banking model into Grameen II, which was fundamentally different, and his change of focus from microcredit to social business.

The fifth pattern of action that undergirds Yunus's success is his constant innovation. He has fearlessly challenged conventional wisdom and been willing to try out new ideas on the basis of his intuition. His trial-and-error approach, and the huge number of ideas that he came up with, resulted in a fair number of failures—but the sheer quantity of his ideas meant he created an enormous trail of successes.

Embedding his values into the cultures of all his organizations is the sixth pattern of action. Yunus created practices and policies to ensure that simplicity, integrity, and hard work were not only his personal values, but the way of life in every Grameen organization. This stands in stark contrast to most Bangladeshi organizations, where lavish perks and corruption have been the order of the day. Therefore, I find it particularly ironic and quite unjust that he has faced charges of fraud and wrongdoing. All the people whom I have talked with about this issue have no doubts about his integrity and believe, as I do, that he has been the victim of political persecution.

The Change-Maker's Roadmap – Lessons from Muhammad Yunus

1. Set forth a compelling vision and stick with it.

2. Communicate relentlessly within and beyond your organization.

3. Build a team that owns your dream.

4. Be flexible.

5. Innovate boldly and do not be afraid to defy conventional wisdom.

6. Embed your values into the organizational culture.

7. Brand yourself and your organization.

The last of Yunus's patterns of action is the way he has been able to brand himself and his organization. He has had the drive and the stamina to keep proclaiming his core message over many years. His story of how he loaned $27 to 42 poor people has become legendary. His passionate speeches about his bank and microcredit have made Grameen a word that is recognized around the planet. His cohesive and powerful narrative about eliminating poverty has changed not only the way millions of people look at this issue but also how they behave.

*　*　*　*　*

The Harvard Business School students sit on the grass under the blossoming trees, enjoying the unexpected warmth of the April sunshine. It is 2012 and months have passed since Yunus was ousted from the Grameen Bank. At four o'clock the crowd begins to pour into the auditorium. Eventually there are more than 1,100 of them, a huge crowd for an afternoon talk, and they mirror the diversity of the planet. As I walk into the building, I chat with a young Korean man who has just left a finance job to go to work for a non-profit. The Brazilian woman sitting next to me has worked for a microfinance organization in Brazil, and she tells me how they modified the Grameen model to fit their situation. On my other side sits a young woman from Finland, an undergraduate at Harvard, who will work this summer at a think-tank in London exploring alternative forms of microfinance.

Yunus launches into his vintage lecture about the $27, about eliminating poverty, about social business. My practiced ear catches a few new twists. Today he is highlighting healthcare and sustainable services. He talks about how science fiction foreshadowed the advances we have made in technology, and now he says we need a social fiction to help us envision a better world in terms of human experience. He doesn't mention that he has left the Grameen Bank or talk about the uncertainties that he faces in Bangladesh. He is looking ahead to new ventures and all the work that lies ahead.

As he finishes, the students rise to their feet and give him a long standing ovation. They clap because he is their hero. They know he has flung open the doors of financial services to the world's poor and that he is still deeply engaged in changing the world for the better. And they clap because they will walk in his footsteps and be the ones who will change the world tomorrow.

Note on Bangladeshi Names

Readers may be confused about the names of the Bangladeshis in this book. Many people in Bangladesh have only one name while others have a given name and a family name. People in the same family may not share a family name as is the case with Muhammad Yunus and his siblings, although today the use of family names is becoming more common. Often women who have only a single name are referred to as so and so Begum or so and so Khatun. This looks like a last name to an American, but in reality, it is a title somewhat similar to Mrs or Madam.

I have chosen to refer to the Bangladeshi people whom I met according to how I and others addressed them rather than to be consistent. Some I called by their last names while others I called by their first names. Thus I refer to Latifee because that is how I and others addressed him, but I call Lamiya Morshed, Lamiya, and Mafuz Anam is always referred to by both names.

Twenty-Seven Dollars and a Dream

Acknowledgments

Many thanks to all the people I interviewed for this book. First and foremost are those in Bangladesh who shared their knowledge and insights about Muhammad Yunus and the Grameen Bank with me: Mahfuz Anam, K.M. Ashaduzzaman, S.M. Shamim Anwar, Anish Barua, Jafar Ullah Bhuyan, Bishaka Rana Das, Muhammad Ibrahim, Muhammad Jahangir, Abser Kamal, H.I. Latifee, Shiban Mahbub, Nasir Ali Mamun, Minara Begum, Golam Morshed Mohammed, Hafiz Mujahid, Nurjahan Begum, Jannat-E- Quanine, A.B.M. Mustafizur Rahaman, Mukhlesur Rahman, M. Shahjahan, Shapna Begum, Sharmeen Shehabuddin, Imamus Sultan. I am especially appreciative of Lamiya Morshed who scheduled my interviews with Professor Yunus and dozens of others at the Grameen Bank and other Grameen organizations.

I am indebted to all those I interviewed here in the United States and also in France, Germany, Spain. Thanks to David Bornstein, Daniel Brodhead, Saskia Bruysten, Rolf Carriere, Michael Chu, Alex Counts, Asif Dowla, Sam Daley-Harris, Susan Davis, Sean Foote, John Hatch, Isabelle Heliot, Hans Herren, Mary Houghton, Dean Karlen, Yan Li, Sam Mitchell, Jonathan Morduch, Holly Mosher, Barbara

Parfitt, Benoit Ringot, David Roodman, Lillian Steinhaeser, Michaela Walsh, Kim Wilson. I am especially grateful to Vidar Jorgensen for his ongoing support of this project.

My deepest appreciation goes to Professor Yunus who gave me many hours of his time and who shared so many reflections of his life with me. Without his cooperation, this book could not have been written.

Then there is my family. From my father I learned the importance of economics and history, to care about social justice and not to believe something just because it was in the newspaper. From my mother I learned about writing as a craft. My four sons and four daughters-in-law – Dan and Elizabeth Esty, Paul and Vanda Esty, Ben Esty and Raquel Leder, and Jed Esty and Andrea Goulet – have provided encouragement throughout the years. Special thanks to my son Ben, who was quick to spot Yunus in the news and who sent me dozens of useful links and articles.

A million thanks to John, my husband, for being there to support me when I needed it and for cheerfully accepting my long hours behind closed doors while I worked on this book.

Then to my many teachers about social justice and women's empowerment. I am grateful to them all – my fellow members of NTL, my former colleagues at Ibis Consulting Group and to the many social activists at First Parish, Concord.

Then there are those who assisted me with the writing, editing and rewriting of this book. My Writing Group generously contributed their ideas, their wildly differing perspectives and their editing skills to improve this book, chapter by chapter: Jeanine Calabria, Sue Curtin, Becky Sue Epstein, Fran Grigsby, Maile Houlihan, Barbara Lynn-Davis, Marti Thomas and Elisabeth Townsend. Sue Rardin and Liesl Schillinger helped with the editing and provided a host of suggestions. And thanks to Elena Petricone and Ken Lizotte who shepherded me through the final process of getting this book published. I am grateful for their efforts, insights and steadiness.

And finally, thanks to Cindy Murphy for her expert assistance with the book's layout and design.

Twenty-Seven Dollars and a Dream

Notes

Chapter 1

1. Ole Danbolt Mjos, announcement of the Nobel Peace Prize, October 1, 2006, www.nobelprize.org.

2. Tom Bethell, *The American*, May/June 2007:34 (7).

3. Satterthwaite, David. "Nobel Prize Links Microfinance to Peace." Bill Baue. *Social Funds.* www.Socialfunds.com/news/article.cgi/2139.html.

4. Yunus, interview with author, January 19, 2010.

5. Ole Danbolt Mjos, Nobel Peace Prize presentation speech, 2006. www.nobelprize.org.

6. Democracy Now Online. www.democracynow.org. 13 December 2006.

7. Yunus, interview with author, January 19, 2010.

8. Yunus, interview with author, January 19, 2010.

Chapter 2

1. Muhammad Ibrahim, interview with author, January 13, 2010.

2. Yunus, interview with author, January 19, 2010.

3. Yunus, interview with author, January 19, 2010.

4. Muhammad Ibrahim, interview with author, January 13, 2010.

5. Muhammad Ibrahim, interview with author, January 13, 2010.

6. Yunus, (1999), 12.

7. Yunus, interview with author, January 19, 2010.

Chapter 3

1. Yunus, interview with author, January 19, 2010.

2. Yunus, interview with author, January 19, 2010.

3. Counts, (2008), 33.

4. Yunus, interview with author, January 19, 2010.

5. Yunus, interview with author, January 19, 2010.

6. Yunus, interview with author, January 19, 2010.

7. Yunus, interview with author, January 19, 2010.

8. Yunus interview with author, January 19, 2010.

9. Yunus interview with author, January 19, 2010.

10. Yunus interview with author, January 19, 2010.

11. Yunus, (1999), 21.

Chapter 4

1. Yunus, interview with author, January 19, 2010.
2. Yunus, interview with author, January 19, 2010.
3. Yunus, interview with author, January 19, 2010.
4. Yunus, interview with author, January 19, 2010.
5. H.I. Latifee, interview with author, January 12, 2010.
6. Anish Barua, interview with author, January 15, 2010.
7. H.I. Latifee, interview with author, January 12, 2010.
8. H.I. Latifee, interview with author, January 12, 2010.
9. Bornstein, (1996), 34-35.
10. Yunus, interview with author, January 19, 2010.
11. H.I. Latifee, interview with author, January 12, 2010.
12. Yunus, interview with author, January 19, 2010

Chapter 5

1. Yunus, interview with author, January 19, 2010.
2. Yunus, interview, with author, January 20, 2010.
3. Yunus, interview, with author, January 20, 2010.
4. Yunus, (1999), 54.

Chapter 6

1. Nurjahan, interview with author, January 14, 2010.

2. Bornstein, (1996), 56.

3. Nurjahan, interview with author, January 14, 2010.

4. Yunus, interview with author, January 20, 2010.

5. Yunus, interview, with author, January 20, 2010.

6. Yunus, interview, with author, January 20, 2010.

7. Nurjahan, interview with author, January 14, 2010.

8. Nurjahan, interview with author, January 14, 2010.

9. Counts, (2008), 66.

10. Bornstein, (1996), 128.

11. Bornstein, (1996), 129.

Chapter 7

1. Lamiya Morshed, interview with author, January 10, 2010.

2. Yunus, interview with author, January 20, 2010.

3. Yunus, (1999), 8.

4. Yunus, (1999), 135.

5. Yunus, interview with author, January 20, 2010.

6. Counts, (2008), 12.

7. Counts, (2008) 105ff and 199ff.

8. Yunus, interview with author, January 20, 2010.

9. Yunus, interview with author, January 20, 2010.

10. Todd, (1996), 223.

11. Bornstein, (1996), 144.

Chapter 8

1. H.I. Latifee, interview with author, January 12, 2010.
2. H.I. Latifee, interview with author, January 12, 2010.
3. H.I. Latifee, interview with author, January 12, 2010.
4. Yunus, interview with author, January 20, 2010.
5. Yunus, interview with author, January 20, 2010.
6. Asif Dowla, interview with author, October 3, 2009.
7. Asif Dowla, interview with author, October 3, 2009.
8. Yunus, interview with author, January 20, 2010.
9. Yunus, interview with author, January 20, 2010.
10. Yunus, interview with author, January 20, 2010.
11. Yunus, interview with author, January 20, 2010.
12. Bornstein, (1996), 167.
13. Yunus, interview with author, January 20, 2010.
14. Yunus, interview with author, January 20, 2010.
15. Yunus, interview with author, January 20, 2010.
16. Yunus, interview with author, January 20, 2010.

Chapter 9

1. Bornstein, (1996) 176.

2. Yunus, interview with author, January 20, 2010.

3. Novak, (1993), 248.

4. Yunus, interview with author, January 20, 2010.

5. Yunus, interview with author, January 20, 2010.

6. Mary Houghton, interview with author, August 8, 2009.

7. Bornstein, (1996), 254.

8. Yunus, (1999), 207.

9. Bornstein, (1996), 240.

10. Bornstein, (1996), 239.

Chapter 10

1. "Iqbal Quadir – Opportunity Comes Calling." *Asiaweek*, 6 July 2001.

2. Yunus, interview with author, August 29, 2010.

3. Richard Shaffer, "Unplanned Obsolescence." *Fast Company.* 1 September 2007. http://www.fastcompany.com/magazine/118/unplanned-obsolescence.html.

4. Vidar Jorgensen, interview with author, September 10, 2011.

Chapter 11

1. Yunus, speech at 1997 Microcredit Summit, www.grameencentre.

2. Todd, (1996b), 102.

3. Yunus (1999b), 178.

4. John Hatch, interview with author, October 28, 2011.

5. Sam Daley-Harris, interview with author, November 30, 2011.

6. Yunus (1999), 256.

7. Yunus, speech at 1997 Microcredit Summit, www.grameencentre.

8. Yunus, speech at 1997 Microcredit Summi, www.grameencentre.

9. Hatch, interview with author, November 30, 2011.

10. Bruck, Connie. "Millions for Millions." *New Yorker.* 30 October 2006.

11. Bruck, Connie. "Millions for Millions." *New Yorker.* 30 October 2006.

Chapter 12

1. Yunus, (2007), xvi.
2. Benoit Ringot, interview with author. December 21, 2011.
3. *Microfinance Focus*, special ed. 2011, 32. www.microfinancefocus.com.
4. Yunus, (2010), xiv.
5. Yunus, interview with author January 20, 2010.
6. Saskia Bruysten, interview with author, December 16, 2011.
7. Saskia Bruysten, interview with author, December 16, 2011.
8. Isabelle Heliot, interview with author December 21, 2011.
9. Benoit Ringot, interview with author, December 21, 2011.
10. Yunus, interview with author, August 29, 2010.
11. Yunus, interview with author, August 29, 2010.
12. Yunus, (2010), xx.
13. Gladwell, Malcolm, "Creation Myth," *New Yorker*, 1 May 2010.

Chapter 13

1. "Bangladesh", *Weekly News Digest*, April 4-11, 2011

2. Mafuz Anam, interview with author, January 20, 2010.

3. Mafuz Anam, interview with author, January 20, 2010.

4. Mafuz Anam, interview with author, January 20, 2010.

5. Mafuz Anam, interview with author, January 20, 2010.

6. Mafuz Anam, interview with author, January 20, 2010.

7. Yunus, interview with author, August 29, 2010.

8. Yunus, interview with author, August 29, 2010.

9. Yunus, interview with author, August 29, 2010.

10. Polgreen, Lydia. "Nobel Laureate Loses Last Legal Battle to Save Job at Bank." *New York Times*, 6 April 2000.

11. Saskia Bruysten, interview with author, December 16, 2011.

12. Saskia Bruysten, interview with author, December 16, 2011.

13. Denyer, Simon. "U.S. Deeply Troubled as Bangladesh Tries to Remove Nobel Laureate As Bank Chief." *Washington Post*. 3 March 2011.

14. Denyer, Simon. "U.S. Deeply Troubled as Bangladesh Tries to Remove Nobel Laureate. As Bank Chief. *Washington Post*. 3 March 2011.

15. "Bangladesh Resumes Microfinance Laureate Hearings" *The Free Library*. www.thefreelibrary.com. AFP Global Ed. 7 March 2011.

16. Polgreen, Lydia. "Microcredit Pioneer Faces an Inquiry in Bangladesh." *New York Times*. Asia Pacific. 29 January 2011.

17. Bornstein, David. "Microfinance Under Fire." *New York Times*, 21 March 2011.

18. Saskia Bruysten, interview with author, December 16, 2011.

19. "Nobel Laureate in Bangladesh Defamation Case." *Worldnews*. 18 January 2011.

20. Michaela Walsh, interview with author, October 7, 2010.

Chapter 14

1. Yunus, (2007), 111.

2. Mordach, Jonathan. "Does Microfinance Really Help the Poor? New Evidence from Flagship Programs in Bangladesh." Draft manuscript, February 26, 1998.

3. Pearl, Daniel and Michael Phillips. "Grameen Bank, which Pioneered Loans for the Poor, Has Hit a Repayment Snag." *Wall Street Journal*, 27 November 2001.

4. Sinha, Sanjay. "The Year of Microfinance Bashing." *Economic Times*, 17 August 2006.

5. Yunus, interview with the author, August 29, 2010.

6. David Roodman's Microfinance Open Book Blog, July 29, 2010.

7. "Microcredit in India is Imperiled by Defaults." *New York Times*, 25 November 2010.

8. Bajaj, Vikas. "In India, SKS Microfinance Reflects Industry's Troubles." *New York Times* Online. May 2011. www.nytimes.com/2011/05/11/business.

9. Sinha, Sanjay. "What the World Can Learn from the Indian Microfinance Crisis" *Microfinance Focus*, special ed. 2011, 26.

10. "Interview with Nathanael Goldberg." Philanthropy Action. 6 September 2009. www.philanthropyaction.com.

11. Bennett, Drake. "Small Change." *Boston Globe*, 20 September, 2009. www.poverty-action.org/node/2256.

12. Bennett, Drake. "Small Change." *Boston Globe*, 20 September, 2009.

13. David Roodman, interview with author, March 12, 2012.

Chapter 15

1. Jahangir, interview with author, March 12, 2012.

2. Barbara Parfitt, interview with author, April 20, 2012.

3. Lamiya Morshed, interview with author, February 7, 2012.

4. Yunus, interview with author, April 20, 2012.

5. Michael Chu, interview with author, April 17, 2012.

6. Michael Chu, interview with author, April 17, 2012.

Twenty-Seven Dollars and a Dream

References

Banerjee, Abhijit V. and Duflo, Esther. *Poor Economics: A Radical Rethinking of the Way to Fight Global Poverty.* New York: Public Affairs, 2011.

Bornstein, David. *How to Change the World: Social Entrepreneurs and the Power of New Ideas.* New York: Oxford University Press, 2007.

Bornstein, David. *The Price of a Dream: The Story of the Grameen Bank.* New York: Simon &Schuster, 1996.

Bruck, Connie. "Millions for Millions. A Reporter at Large." *New Yorker Magazine,* 30 October 2006.

Counts, Alex. *Give Us Credit: How Muhammad Yunus's Micro-Lending Revolution is Empowering Women from Bangladesh to Chicago.* New York: Times Books/Random House, 1996.

Counts, Alex. *Small Loans, Big Dreams: How Nobel Prize Winner Muhammad Yunus and Microfinance are Changing the World.* Hoboken, NJ: John Wiley and Sons, Inc., 2008.

Daley-Harris, Sam and Awimbo, Anna, Eds. *More Pathways Out of Poverty.* Bloomfield, CT: Kumerian Press, 2006.

Daley-Harris, Sam, Ed. *Pathways Out of Poverty: Innovations in Microfinance for the Poorest Families.* Bloomfiield, CT: Kumerian Press, 2002.

Davis, Susan and Khosha Vinod. "Taking Stock of the Microcredit Summit Campaign, What Worked and What Didn't Work 1997-2006? What is Needed 2007-2015?" Paper available at http:/papers.ssrn.com id=978862

Esty, Katharine. "Lessons from Muhammad Yunus and the Grameen Bank: Leading Long-term Organizational Change Successfully." *OD Practitioner* Vol.43 No.1 2011:24.

Fuglesang, Andreas and Chandler, Dale. *Participation as Process–Process as Growth–and What We Can Learn from Grameen Bank Bangladesh.* Dhaka: Grameen Trust, 1993.

Holcombe, Susan. *Managing to Empower: The Grameen Bank's Experience of Poverty Alleviation.* London: Zed Books, 1995.

Islam, Aminul A.K.M. *A Bangladesh Village: Political Conflict and Cohesion.* Prospect Heights, IL: Waveland Press, 1974.

Larance, Lisa Young. "Fostering Social Capital Through NGO Design: Grameen Bank Membership in Bangladesh." *International Social Work.* 2001 44: 7-18.

Mordach, Jonathan. "Does Microfinance Really Help the Poor? New Evidence from Flagship Programs in Bangladesh." Draft manuscript, 26 February 1998.

Morshed, Lamiya. "Lessons Learned in Improving
Replicability of Successful Microcredit Programs – How
Can the Best Models 'Travel Better.'" Paper, Grameen
Trust, Bangladesh.

Sample, Bob. "How RESULTS Activist Collaborated with
Microcredit Leaders and High Government Officials to
Build the Microfinance Movement." Paper prepared for
the Global Microcredit Summit 2006 in Halifax, Canada.
2006.

Spiegel, Peter and Richter, Roger. *The Power of Dignity:
The Grameen Family.* Bielefeld, Germany: J.Kamphausen,
2008.

Todd, Helen. *Women at the Center: Grameen Bank
Borrowers after One Decade.* Boulder, CO: Westview
Press, 1996.

Todd, Helen, Ed. *Cloning Grameen Bank: Replicating a
Poverty Reduction Model in India, Nepal and Vietnam.*
London: IT Publications, 1996.

Wahid, Abu N.M., Ed. *The Grameen Bank: Poverty
Relief in Bangladesh.* Boulder, CO: Westview Press, 1993.

Yunus, Muhammad. *Banker to the Poor: Micro-lending
and the Battle against World Poverty.* New York: Public
Affairs, 1999.

Yunus, Muhammad. *Creating a World Without Poverty:
Social Business and the Future of Capitalism.* New
York: Public Affairs, 2007.

Yunus, Muhammad. *Grameen Bank at a Glance.* Dhaka: Grameen Bank, 2008.

Yunus, Muhammad. *Building Social Businesses: The New Kind of Capitalism that Serves Humanity's Most Pressing Needs.* New York: Public Affairs, 2010.

Twenty-Seven Dollars and a Dream

Videos and Web Sites

To Catch a Dollar: Muhammad Yunus Banks on America. Dir. Gayle Ferraro. Aerial Productions, 2009. DVD. www.tocatchadollar.com.

The Yunus Centre. 26 Dec 2012 www.muhammadyunus.org

Muhammad Yunus: Banker to the Poor. The Social Entrepreneurship Series. Ashoka's Global Academy for Social Entrepreneurship, 2006. DVD.

The Official Website of the Nobel Prize. Nobelprize.org. 26 Dec 2012 http://www.nobelprize.org

Pennies a Day. izzit.org. DVD.

Bonsai People: The Vision of Muhammad Yunus. Dir. Holly Mosher. FilmBuff, 2012. DVD.

Small Fortunes: Microcredit and the Future of Poverty. Prod. BYU Broadcasting, 2005. DVD.

Twenty-Seven Dollars and a Dream

Index

Twenty-Seven Dollars and a Dream

About the Author

Katharine Esty, a social psychologist, organizational consultant, writer, and psychotherapist, served for twenty years as managing partner of Ibis Consulting Group. While at Ibis, a diversity and organizational effectiveness firm, she consulted to corporations, universities and international

Katharine Esty

agencies in the areas of managing change, women's empowerment, leadership and strategic planning. She first met Muhammad Yunus when she was in Bangladesh consulting to UNICEF. Her previous books are *The Gypsies: Wanderers in Time* and *Workplace Diversity*. Katharine Esty lives in Concord, Massachusetts with her husband, John.

Twenty-Seven Dollars and a Dream

For More Information

For more information about Katharine Esty

katharine.esty@MuhammadYunusToday.com

For more information about Muhammad Yunus

www.muhammadyunus.org

info@yunuscentre.org

Yunus Centre
Global Headquarters
Grameen Bank Tower, 16th floor
Mirpur 2, Dhake-1216
Bangladesh

Telephone (from the USA)
011 8802 903 5755

CPSIA information can be obtained at www.ICGtesting.com
Printed in the USA
LVOW05s1439120114

369107LV00016B/561/P